HURON COUNTY LIBRARY
3 6492 00391565 6

D1115727

Whales of the West Coast

By David A.E. Spalding

HARBOUR PUBLISHING

Published by
HARBOUR PUBLISHING
P.O. Box 219
Madeira Park, BC Canada
V0N 2H0

Cover design and page composition by Roger Handling, Terra Firma Digital Arts
Edited by Susan Mayse
Map by Kevin Oke and Roger Handling
Printed in Canada

Harbour Publishing acknowledges the financial support of the Government of Canada through the Book Publishing Industry Development Program (BPIDP) and the Canada Council for the Arts, and the Province of British Columbia through the British Columbia Arts Council, for its publishing activities.

Canadian Cataloguing in Publication Data

Spalding, David A. E., 1937-
Whales of the west coast

Includes bibliographical references and index.
ISBN 1-55017-199-2

1. Whales—Pacific Coast (North America) I. Title.
QL737.C4S62 1999 599.5′0979 C99-910313-X

Photo, previous page:
A baby humpback stays close to its mother. (Ellis/Ursus)

For Andrea
Who has shared the whales, and so much else.

Acknowledgements

This book has been prepared with the enthusiastic participation of Harbour Publishing's Howard White, Mary White, Peter Robson and Mary Schendlinger, impeccable and imaginative editing by Susan Mayse and striking design by Roger Handling.

Many people have contributed to this book through extensive publication, helpful interviews (often at inconvenient times), provision of specific information, loan of publications and photographs, and provision of accommodation, meals, connections and transportation. First our thanks go to all those whose interviews are featured in the book and whose assistance has often extended far beyond the text. Extensive help has also been provided by numerous photographers, not only those whose work has been used.

Others whose assistance has been invaluable include Mary Abbot (BC Ferries), Rebecca Andrews (Burke Museum), Ed Andrusiak and Sherry O'Hara (Nanaimo), Kelly Balcomb-Bartok (Friday Harbor), Robin Baird (Hawaii), Janet Boon (Alert Bay), Jim Borrowman (Telegraph Cove), Barbara Bryant (Tofino), Darlene Cadwallader (Port McNeill), Brian Compton (Vancouver), Steven Dennis (Tofino), Maurice Fouquette (Coal Harbour), Nicky Graham (Hornby Island), Jim Griffin (UK), Nancy and David Hanson (Friday Harbor), Rick Harbo (Nanaimo) Pat Hole (Coal Harbour), Bill Holm (Burke Museum), Patrick Keen (Wales), Nikki Laine-Mayor (Tofino), Jock Mardres (Edmonton), Brent and Judy Marsden (Pender Island), Bill and Donna McKay, Jarret Morton (Telegraph Cove), Don Newell (Saturna), Cheryl Oke (Pender Island), Rod Palm (Tofino), Calvor Palmateer (Sidney), Penny Rennick (Alaska Geographic), Bernard Ross (Vancouver), Bill Sarjeant (Saskatoon), Mike Sato (Seattle), Susan Schultz (Olympic National Park), Elsa Spalding (UK), Cindy Stokes (Atlanta), Sandra Swetsing (Tofino), Roy Tanami (Vancouver), James Taylor (Alert Bay), Joan Thornley (Vancouver Maritime Museum), AnnaMaria Valastro (Vancouver), Judy Walker (Pender Island), Marlene Whitmore (Sointula), Linda Williamson (Tourism British Columbia), Diane Woodman (Victoria) and Skip Young (Vancouver).

TABLE OF CONTENTS

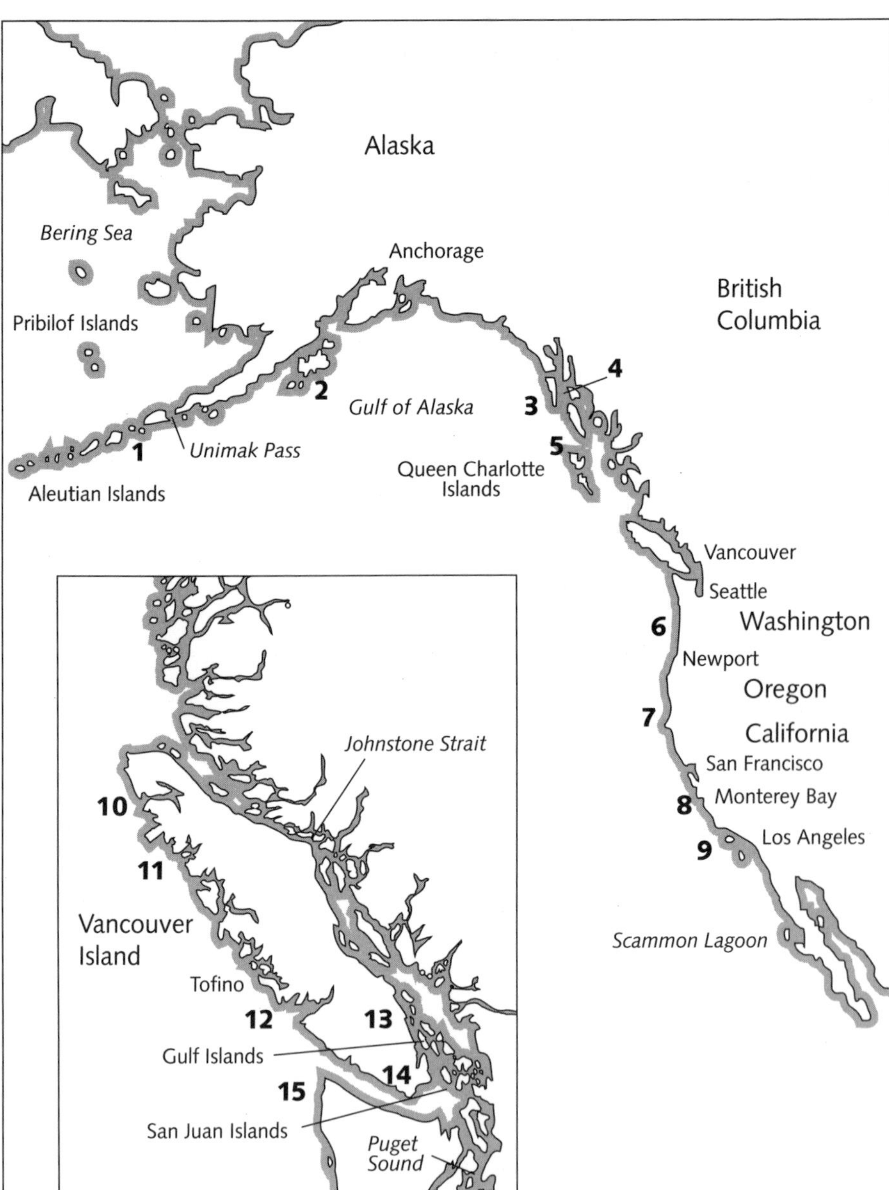

Whaling Stations
1 Akutan
2 Port Hobron
3 Port Armstrong
4 Murder Cove
5 Naden Harbour
6 Gray's Harbour
7 Eureka
8 Monterey
9 San Luis Obispo
10 Coal Harbour
11 Kyuquot
12 Sechart
13 Page's Lagoon
14 Victoria
15 Neah Bay

Aquariums
Vancouver
Newport
Monterey Bay

Museums
Vancouver
Sidney
San Juan Islands

Marine Parks
Johnstone Strait

Parks
Tofino

Beyond Whale Watching

A spyhopping killer whale. (Morton)

On a breezy spring day, our boat is butting the rollers off the west coast of Vancouver Island. Sea surrounds us except to the east, where beyond the rocky coast, green forests climb from the mountain slopes into gray clouds. We are drifting on the track of one of the longest mammal migrations known, waiting to intersect with a passing gray whale. In the heaving swell, a distant spout alerts us to our first whale. As we follow, it emerges again, curving gently out of the water. We briefly glimpse a knobby spine as it rolls its 40-foot body back below the surface again.

More than 20,000 gray whales migrate along the west coast of North America. (Dennis)

We are bobbing offshore in a region where people have a special relationship with whales. From tropical breeding lagoons in distant Baja California, the grays make their deliberate way north past Washington and Oregon, along coasts where First Nations whalers once awaited their coming with dugout canoe and 18-foot lance. Northwest of here the grays leave the coast, crossing paths with humpbacks leaving Hawaii for the more sheltered waters of southern Alaska. There, in the Kodiak Ground, as whalers called it, hundreds of whaling ships once decimated the right whale.

The open Pacific—the biggest part of our one world-spanning ocean—has been home to a multitude of whales through tens of millions of years. Even after the relentless pursuit of big whales and the incidental slaughter of smaller ones, many species still inhabit the offshore waters.

East of Vancouver Island and other coastal islands, a complex of fjords, sounds and straits finger the coastline from Alaska to Puget Sound. Despite extensive persecution and heavy vessel traffic, several whale species, including the world's best known populations of orcas, still shelter here.

Why whales?

Whales, though among our most important and interesting animals, have been little studied until recently.

Whale catchers' guns rang out across the Pacific for most of this century. (VMM)

Almost a third of about seventy living cetacean species have been recorded in North American Pacific coast waters. A rich haul of fossil whales is also gradually emerging from the region's rocks, giving new clues to the origins and development of the group.

All whales belong to the order Cetacea; we collectively call them cetaceans. Science divides them into two groups: a smaller group of great whales which use a variety of filter-feeding techniques with the aid of baleen, and a larger group of generally smaller toothed whales which eat active prey such as fish, squid and other mammals.

The largest cetacean is the impressive 100-foot, 160-ton blue whale; the smallest whales are built nearer to human scale. Experts know some species so intimately that they can name an individual and its specific genealogy, while we know other groups so poorly that we named a new species in the region—Hubbs' beaked whale—as recently as 1963.

Although the earliest naturalists studied whales, much of our knowledge comes from our last few decades of research. We know the toothed whales in particular have a complex social structure and a remarkable degree of intelligence which some claim exceeds our own. Yet new answers raise new questions; we still do not understand everything about even the best-known whales.

Whales and people

Archaeology suggests an aboriginal whaling tradition dating back 3,000 years on the West Coast. The First Peoples' courageous pursuit of grays and humpbacks from dugout canoes has commanded admiration for two centuries. Later, in the ultimate exploitive industry, men of great courage and stamina pursued large whales to the ends of the earth. Commercial whaling in the north Pacific started late by world standards, since the home ports of Atlantic whalers were far distant. Nevertheless, whales were taken by both small rowing boats launched from sailing ships and steam catchers serving factory ships. Shore whaling from Vancouver Island factories continued to 1967.

A great diversity of whale-derived products through history have fed humans, lubricated the industrial revolution and illuminated high society evenings and the work of great writers. They have been trivialized into corset stays, buggy whips, perfume and dog food. Whaling drew researchers to study living whales from catcher ships and to measure and anatomize their carcasses on flensing decks.

Whale bones stacked at Sechart whaling station on Vancouver Island, shown here around 1905, were boiled to extract oil at the end of each season. (BCARS 65536)

A revolution shook the relationship between whales and people in 1964 when the Vancouver Aquarium captured its first orca off Saturna Island and briefly kept it in a tank. Captured north Pacific whales were soon in demand for aquaria around the world. A whale catching industry was in full swing before governments began to question its impact on wild populations and eventually ended the trade.

Scientists leaped at the chance to study living whales, and their research on wild and aquarium whales led to a boom in orca studies. After two decades, researchers can identify individual whale pods by sight and sound, tracking their movements and relationships. Yet even the world's best-known population of marine mammals constantly surprises us; new groups appear and new behaviour patterns evolve.

This research offers whales a brighter future, while archaeology pushes deeper into the past our understanding of aboriginal whaling, and palaeontology increases our knowledge of fossil whales.

Our obsessive hunt of cetaceans has given way to a comprehensive worldwide effort to conserve an international resource. The balance of power changed when small, Vancouver-based Greenpeace shifted its protest from nuclear disarmament to whale conservation. This sparked international public concern for the protection of all whales, which has (for now) closed down most industrial whaling.

The skeleton of this Minke whale was, in 1940, the first to be exhibited in British Columbia. (McTaggart-Cowan)

 Enjoying whales

Among the complex coastal First Nations cultures, whales have filled an important imaginative role. Long ago only chiefs could hunt whales; today whales again play a significant part in resurgent Native arts and culture. In wider society, nonthreatening enjoyment of whales has grown steadily at aquaria and on whale watching expeditions. Public interest has also made possible whale watching parks, protection of key sites, and creation of museums featuring marine mammals.

West Coast whales lay at the heart of two recent ethical controversies. The Makah of Washington state resumed aboriginal whaling, and Keiko—star of the *Free Willy* movies—left his multimillion dollar Oregon facility for Iceland and perhaps eventual

A gray whale was carved on this First Nations pole, seen in Stanley Park in Vancouver. (DAES)

return to the wild. Whales figure increasingly in folk and popular arts, forming the subject matter of oral stories, mass market novels and movies. Their images appear everywhere in West Coast design from business logos to tattoos. Interest in whales extends into the elite culture of paintings, prints and sculptures, and an extensive nonfiction literature. Whales have inspired musical arrangement and composition in several genres; actual whale sounds often add to human-produced music.

This expanding interest draws in people whose lives revolve around cetaceans. Scientists work for governments, universities or other institutions; others keep their research afloat with grants and other support. Keepers or vets and their support staff care for captive whales. Aquarium, museum and park staff, and skippers and crews of whale watching boats, inform and educate the public. Conservationist members of Greenpeace and other groups, and many creative people—photographers, painters, writers and sculptors—interpret whales in their own ways. Whale people (you'll read about several in this book) are as fascinating as whales.

To many people, whales are now the focus of a diffuse mystical cult incorporating ancient wisdom, ideas from afar and interpretations of modern scientific findings that the scientists themselves might not recognize. Some see whales as universally friendly to humans, leading us to a new environmental consciousness. In this swirl of ideas we can recognize an emerging whale culture, in which whales have actual—or at least symbolic—importance in our society. And if closer association with whales can help us develop a new, more intimate, friendly relationship with nature, we surely need it.

Whale watching hot spot

The West Coast is now a whale watching hot spot, bringing tens of thousands of travellers from as far as Japan, Germany, New Zealand and Norway. Pacific Northwest whales have drawn tourists since the early 1900s at least. Today whale watching has considerable economic impact—up to $6 million a year for

A bull orca can be recognized by its six-foot dorsal fin. (Baird)

Oregon, Washington, British Columbia and Alaska—and provides full- and part-time work for many people. All elements of society, including our elected representatives, can approve of this aspect of whale appreciation.

Its ultimate value, though, is the opportunity for people to experience wild whales directly. For many observers, whale watching goes beyond mere wildlife viewing: it can offer life-changing contact and empathy with fellow mammals inhabiting an alien world. Many West Coast residents and visitors become fascinated with whales, going beyond whale watching to active participation in whale conservation, science or interpretation.

This book is designed to help any resident or visitor interested in North America's West Coast whales—whether that interest is mild or profound. It will be useful to readers with only a casual interest but also collects widely scattered, hard-to-find information on many aspects of West Coast whales.

Using this book

Although you can read the book from beginning to end, you will also find it interesting to dip in wherever you like. Stories highlighted in boxes offer a quick survey of places to visit or encounters with people closely associated with whales.

Canada uses metric measurements, while the US uses the imperial system. You will find whale dimensions and other measurements given in both. The US short ton is 2,000 pounds; the metric tonne is 2,200 pounds or 1,000 kilograms. Canadian gallons are slightly larger than US gallons.

The first half of the book provides a broad overview of whale natural history, with particular reference to species found in our region. The second half mainly examines human interactions with whales. A reference section follows.

Chapter 2 invites you to meet the whales and explains their origins, types, biology and ecology.

Chapters 3 and 4 introduce the two main groups of whales, the baleen and toothed whales, emphasizing the commonest species.

Chapter 5 deals with the rarer whales, providing more specialized information for experienced whale watchers.

The oldest human interaction with whales is surely whaling, the pursuit of wild whales for human use as food and other products. Chapter 6 describes how First Nations practised whaling on the BC coast and how commercial whaling spread through the Pacific and continued on the northwest coast until late in this century.

For many years, whaling gave scientists their only ready access to whales; Chapter 7 shows how science has evolved from measurement and anatomy into exciting studies of wild whales.

People come from all over the world to watch whales on the west coast. (Dennis)

Population decline due to whaling inspired the modern whale conservation movement. Chapter 8 discusses the successes, issues that excite debate and remaining barriers to ensuring that whales share the seas with future human generations.

Chapter 9 focusses on first-hand experiences through aquaria, land-based watching and whale watching by boat.

Whales have inspired people throughout history and occupy an important place in our culture. Chapter 10 describes many ways to enjoy whales without direct contact with the living animal.

The reference section lists useful information including Whale Words, addresses of relevant agencies, publications and other media. Whales Through Time provides a chronological framework to the whole story, from the earliest times to the most recent discoveries. Through the Seasons is a month-by-month list of when and where whales regularly appear.

The book lists major sites and services which make it possible to see whales in captivity and in the wild; it cannot list all of the many and ever-changing whale watching companies. Instead I suggest where you can go and how you can choose an option that best meets your needs. Examples highlight some of the best experiences available to you in the world of whales; omission of any institution or service does not imply criticism.

Bon voyage when you sail with the whales! Perhaps I'll see you there.

Meet the Whales

A breaching orca can be the highlight of a whale watching trip. (Baird)

As we sail through patchy fog in one of the inlets behind Vancouver Island or off Puget Sound, a loud snort of exhalation punctuates the silence. A few feet away, a couple of tall dorsal fins have quietly emerged, and as we watch, smaller curved fins also appear. The misty blow hangs above them in the still air, blending with the fog. We have encountered the bulls and cows of a pod of orcas (once better known as killer whales), the largest of the common toothed whales in our region.

Bjossa

The easiest way to meet a whale may be in a large public aquarium such as the Vancouver Aquarium in Stanley Park.

Bjossa is a female orca, one of about fifty in captivity around the world. Born in the wild in Icelandic waters, Bjossa was one of half a dozen captured by fishermen. When the aquarium heard of her capture in 1980, it had just lost its first resident orca, Skana, after thirteen years in the aquarium; the male Hyak was its sole representative of the species. Aquarium director Murray Newman hoped to establish an orca breeding colony. Four new orcas were soon on their way from Iceland, two for the aquarium and two for other locations. Greenpeace opposed importing the whales, but the British Columbia Supreme Court rejected its plea. The aquarium named its two orcas Bjossa and Finna, believing both were females, but Bjossa dominated the pair and Finna later proved to be a male. In about four months the new whales were trained to perform with Hyak. The orcas attracted many visitors including Jane Goodall, Louis Leakey and Queen Elizabeth II.

Meet Bjossa, long-term resident of the Vancouver Aquarium. (DAES)

Donations built a new larger pool specifically for orcas. Bjossa's home, an outdoor 880,000-gallon (4 million litre) pool, opened in 1986 with great ceremony. Bjossa gave birth in November 1988—Canada's first orca birth in captivity—but the calf lived only three weeks. In September 1991 she gave birth to a male calf; DNA tests showed that the father was the recently deceased Hyak. The calf was named K'yosha, but despite the best efforts of the aquarium staff, it died of a brain infection after four months.

For fifteen years, Bjossa lived in the aquarium with her male companion Finna. Aquarium staff, reluctantly realizing that they lacked adequate breeding facilities, injected Bjossa with a chemical contraceptive; long-term effects are unknown. Bjossa's hormone levels caused alarm in 1998, but tests showed she was not pregnant.

Under ongoing pressure from a lobby urging the aquarium not to keep any orcas, the board reviewed its policy in June 1995. It acknowledged orcas released to the wild could not be guaranteed to succeed and recognized the importance of showing them to many people unlikely to encounter wild whales. Funds for enlarging the pool would probably not be available, however, so orcas could only be a nonbreeding population. Bjossa will remain but not breed; another captive nonbreeding female would come to keep her company. Finna was offered on loan, but by the late 1990s no other aquarium had taken him. Since orcas do not mate for life, separation was not believed to be cruel. In October 1997, after seventeen years at the aquarium, Finna died of an acute infection.

Wheels and pigfish

Our word *whale* describes glimpses of surfacing cetaceans; its Old English root *hvael* means "a wheel." A large whale's rolling back often looks just like the rim of a wheel revolving below the surface. Humans have watched whales with fascination for a long time. Our names for smaller whales derive from Greek and Roman names. *Dolphin* comes from Latin *delphinus,* while *porpoise* comes ultimately from Latin, meaning "pigfish."

A humpback rolls, showing its small dorsal fin. (Dennis)

Some names are ancient, but since whales are wide ranging and (until recently) little studied, no clearly agreed set of English names exists for particular species.

Though we refer to mainly larger species as whales, for convenience we also call smaller relatives whales—for instance, the 11-foot (3.4 m) pygmy sperm whale, a rare visitor to our waters. You may hear, as I have, that "the killer whale is not a whale but a dolphin." This certainly reflects its relationship, if not normal English usage.

Generally we name cetacean species—about seventy worldwide—by combining *whale, dolphin* or *porpoise* with a term describing their appearance, behaviour, discoverer or region. In our area, for example, we have gray and killer whales, the Pacific

A pod of orcas looming through the mist brings the ocean to life unexpectedly. (Morton R)

white-sided dolphin and Dall's porpoise. In common usage dolphins have a projecting snout and porpoises do not, but there's no universal agreement. Different English names may be used for each species, even in the same region, and many whales occur worldwide. But we are approaching standardization.

This book offers the most widely accepted names for each whale. As you talk with local people, you will find some group and species names in flux. A strong movement favours renaming killer whales to orcas (from their scientific name) to change a misleading public image. Fishermen often ignore both names, however, and continue to call them blackfish.

What makes a whale?

Whales share many anatomical and physiological features of other mammals, but differ greatly in some ways. A close look suggests how they evolved from ancient land mammals ancestral to all furry creatures.

Cetaceans feed their young with milk, as other mammals do, and bear them alive—a feat presenting problems for sea animals that breathe air. Warm-blooded, they maintain a more or less constant temperature. Land mammals can only do this by insulating their bodies from their surroundings; most zoology textbooks give mammals' most obvious characteristic as a covering of hair.

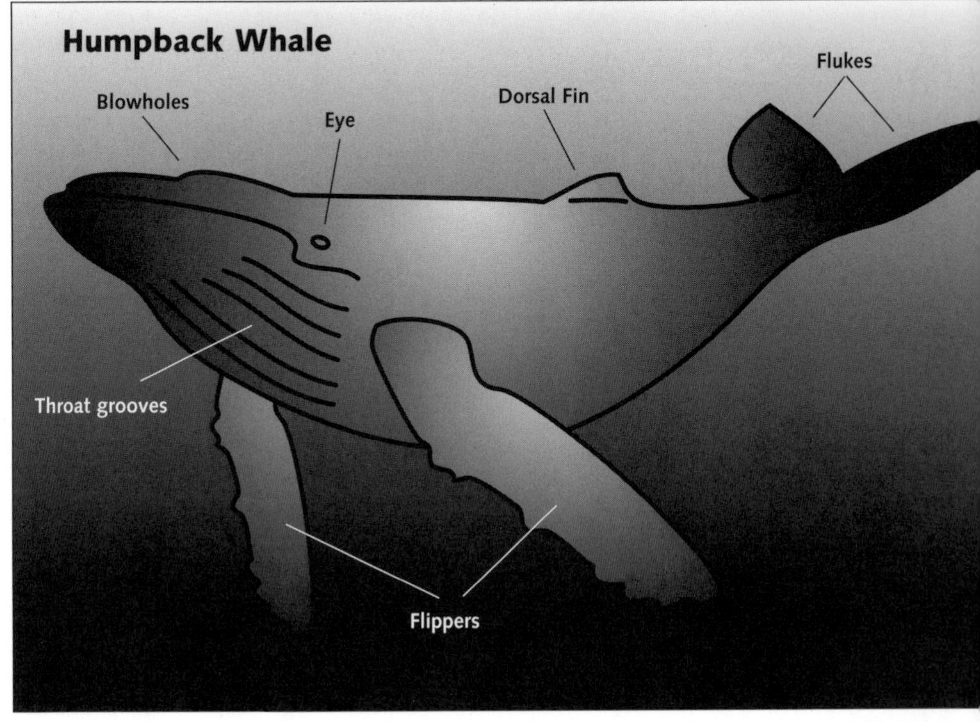

Whales have lost most of their hair, however, along with hind limbs and other appendages, to live in an environment which favours streamlining. You must look hard to find hairs on a whale, but there are usually a few—for instance, gray whales have some isolated hairs on their heads and lower jaws. Instead, a thick blubber layer beneath the skin now provides insulation.

Other adaptations to ocean life include a streamlined body, forelimbs modified into flippers, a wide, flat tail and nostrils opening as a blowhole on top of the head.

While large land mammals need strong skeletons to support them, the bones of whales are usually less dense—think of the spongy texture of Inuit whalebone carvings. Whales' forelimbs have become paddles used more for steering than propulsion. They have evolved by developing a fleshy pad enclosing the bones that in humans support the forearm, wrist, hand and fingers. The hind limbs have essentially disappeared, though whales retain the genetic capacity to produce them. A humpback brought in to the Kyuquot (Vancouver Island) whaling station in 1919 had two hind legs protruding 4 feet (1.2 m) from its body, containing the appropriate bones—traces of a tibia, tarsus and metatarsus—and cartilage for a functioning leg.

Consider the special adaptations that allow cetaceans to live successfully in the ocean. Water is denser than air, thus harder to move through. Human swimmers often increase their thrust by wearing rubber flippers on their feet. Whales have solved the same problem by developing flukes, a broad double flap on the end of the tail. This tail, with no bony base, is largely composed of fibrous ligaments. The whale swims by using powerful back and tail muscles to flap the flukes up and down. Streamlined shape and bare skin (which feels like firm rubber on a living whale) reduce water resistance.

Blubber, a layer of fatty tissue, covers whales beneath their skin. Water conducts heat away from a warm body about twenty-seven times faster than air. (Hypothermia—dangerously low body temperature—is a principal cause of death for people who fall overboard in northwest waters.) Whales too must retain heat in all but the warmest tropical seas. A large body decreases the surface area/volume ratio; this requires the insulation provided by blubber, up to five inches (12 cm) thick in a blue whale. On flukes and flippers, a complex heat exchange mechanism allows veins to recapture heat from arteries.

Whale trivia

For those who want to win bets in the bar or on the boat, here are a few useful whale trivia. Statistics which are maxima for any animal are indicated by an asterisk (*); others are the maxima for cetacea only.

Biggest

*baby—blue—23 feet (7 m)
*baleen—bowhead—14.5 feet (4.5 m)
*brain—sperm whale—22 lbs (10 kg)
*testicles (each)—right whale—1 ton (900 kg)

Deepest

diver—sperm—3,330 feet (1014 m)
*sound—fin and blue—20 hertz

Fastest

baleen whale—sei—30 mph (50 kph)

Longest

gestation period—large Mysticetes—to 12 months
penis—blue whale—10 feet (3 m)

Loudest

*call—blue whale—188 decibels

Most

*baleen plates (average)—fin whale—360
teeth (average)—spinner dolphin—224

Deep breathing

Whales, which breathe air, must take several deep breaths before diving. They have remarkably small lungs—the capacity is only about 3 percent of body weight, whereas ours are more than 6 percent. Cetaceans can store much greater quantities of oxygen in their muscles, however, which appear deeper red than the meat of land mammals. Sperm whales, which feed in deep water, can stay below for half an hour or more—so they must spend a similar period on the surface recovering between dives.

This lifestyle does not work for really small animals—that's why there are no marine equivalents of mice, and the smallest whales live in warm tropical waters. It does work well for porpoises and dolphins that are about human size, perhaps one reason we relate to them so well. As water is more buoyant than air, whales are practically weightless in water and some have developed heavier bodies than land animals can.

On the Pacific coast, we have the largest species and two of the smallest; harbor and Dall's porpoises are around 6 feet (2 m), and the longest blue whale recorded in British Columbia was 86 feet (26.2 m). For years we've said our largest living whale is the largest animal that ever lived, but recent dinosaur discoveries suggest otherwise.

The biggest animal?

Many books claim that the blue whale is "bigger than any dinosaur," sometimes adding that no land animal can grow so large. Indeed, the size of the largest whales boggle the mind. Several immense individual whales have been documented (though some question the dimensions of the largest). The biggest accurately measured blue seems to be a female 109'4" (33.32 m) long taken near the South Shetlands in March 1926. About the same time and place whalers took a male 107'1" (32.64 m) long. The longest documented northern hemisphere individual at 98' (30 m) was killed in the Panama Canal on January 23, 1922.

Measuring the length of a large dead whale is difficult; estimating its weight is almost impossible. One source claimed a recorded maximum of 220 tons (198 tonnes), but a carefully weighed one was 134.2 tons (122 tonnes). Weighing such a large mass of flesh and bone is difficult. The largest were accessible only on flensing decks, after cutting released many gallons of blood. On one occasion, blood and stomach contents were estimated at 9.7 tons (8.8 tonnes)—a significant amount even for so large an animal. It is impossible to verify the disputed measurement of a specimen already carved up and turned into many different products, as whalers unhesitatingly did with the largest creatures ever hunted. Sadly, ongoing whaling prevents specimens from reaching the giant sizes of earlier whales.

A century ago, the heaviest dinosaur known was *Apatosaurus* (Brontosaurus) estimated at 30 tons (27 tonnes), and the longest was the slighter *Diplodocus* at 87 feet (27 m). Today we are discovering still larger sauropods, long-tailed long-necked monsters that many people imagine when they hear "dinosaur." Successive "biggests" have included *Brachiosaurus, Supersaurus, Ultrasaurus* and *Seismosaurus*. The last remarkable beast, known from the rear half of one skeleton, stood between 120 and 150 feet (37 and 45 m) long and weighed around 100 tons (91 tonnes). A recently discovered Cretaceous giant, South America's *Argentinosaurus*, may have stretched even longer. Half-time score: dinos winning on length, whales winning on weight.

Conquering the oceans

Whales are the mammals most successfully adapted for marine life (see comparisons below), but they are only one of many vertebrate "experiments" at conquering the oceans. Most fish species live in the ocean, though there are many freshwater species. Amphibians such as frogs and salamanders live partly in fresh water and partly on land; no marine examples are known. Their descendants, the reptiles, at first were independent of water, but during the Mesozoic, several groups of reptiles moved back into the sea. Of these only marine turtles and saltwater crocodiles have survived into modern times.

Anatomical comparisons show that the ancestors of whales lived on land, though it may be hard to imagine how a terrestrial creature could adapt so well to marine life.

Other West Coast mammals have also adapted more or less successfully to marine living. Though not directly related, they illustrate possible stages of whale adaptation. River otters are wonderful swimmers but also travel freely on land. Sea otters spend all or most of their time in the sea; they catch and eat food, and even produce young, without going to land. Seal and sea lion legs have become flippers; they spend most of their time in the water but still haul out to rest and bear their young.

Whales, along with the unrelated extinct Steller's sea cow and surviving dugongs, are unable to function on land and thus are most completely adapted for the water. Their bodies have become streamlined, and though they still have a pelvis, their front legs have become flippers and they have developed flukes on their tails.

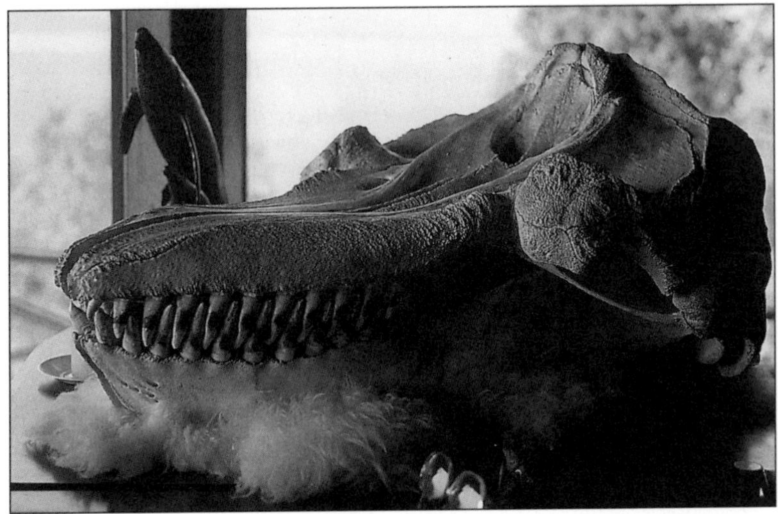

An orca skull shows a mouthful of pointed teeth. (DAES)

In the still mysterious great extinction of all dinosaurs (except those that became birds), most marine reptile groups disappeared. This seems to have left a vacant niche, an oceanic food supply unexploited by land-evolving mammals. About 60 million years ago, primitive mammals called mesonychids in North America and Asia combined features of modern hoofed mammals with wolflike size and teeth and perhaps an omnivorous diet. Some mesonychids remained on land and developed into modern hoofed mammals such as hippopotami, camels, pigs and cattle. Others explored the seashore for food, adapted to life in the water and ultimately left the land to become whales. This apparently unlikely relationship is supported by comparing, for example, the three-chambered stomachs shared by whales, camels and hippos. Recent studies of albumen proteins offer more precise evidence that the whales' closest land relatives are hippopotami and then cattle.

The oldest fossil whales known (around 50 million years), fragmentary skulls from the Eocene of Pakistan, clearly show links between mesonychids and later whales. By the Oligocene (35 million years ago), the two modern groups of toothed and baleen whales were already distinct. Skulls of Oligocene toothed whales suggest that they could echolocate.

Aetiocetus from Oregon is the first known baleen whale, although it still had fully developed adult teeth. (Modern baleen whales have teeth only in the embryonic stage.) Another toothed baleen whale of about the same age, *Chonecetus*, comes from the Sooke Formation of Vancouver Island. Baleen does not fossilize, but extensive blood vessels in the roof of the mouth indicate its presence.

Jim and Gail Goedert – paleowhalers

Jim Goedert and his wife Gail of Gig Harbor, Washington, share an unusual hobby—for eighteen years they have been collecting fossil whales, mainly near Pysht on the south shore of the Strait of Juan de Fuca. Whale skulls and other bones often occur here in concretions in thousands of feet of deep-water marine sediments.

Jim and Gail Goedert (foreground) have spent decades finding fossil whales in the western United States. (Goedert)

Jim and Gail had collected invertebrate fossils for a while when they visited New Zealand. There Ewan Fordyce, a specialist in fossil whales who had done work in the Pacific Northwest, told them about localities in their own backyard. No one had collected seriously, though a few reports mentioned local fossils. Soon they found their first whale material and "now it seems that everywhere we go there are whale bones."

Their finds led to an intensive search, which over years has produced some 400 whale specimens, from single bones to nearly complete skeletons. Most are primitive Odontocetes, some perhaps representing new families, from the upper Eocene and Oligocene.

The fossil hunters received support in 1978 from the University of Washington and later from Larry Barnes, a marine mammal palaeontologist at the Natural History Museum of Los Angeles County, who is impressed with their finds: "Jim and Gail Goedert have collected more fossil whales [from the Oligocene] than all other people in all of recorded history."

The Goederts, despite support from the museum and the National Geographic Society, have done most of their work on their own. The concretions have yielded most material, but they have also excavated with electric jackhammers.

"We're slowing down a bit now," said Jim, "but there's still stuff there. We're still trying to find the stuff before some rockhound beats the concretions to pieces." Apart from the excitement of the chase, there are other rewards. A new fossil whale, *Chonecetus geodertorum*, bears the Goederts' name.

Two feeding strategies

Evolving in the water, whales developed two distinct feeding strategies. Baleen whales (Mysticetes) have lost their teeth and use the giant sieve made of masses of baleen to catch and filter out large amounts of small prey. Some baleen whales take floating plankton; others dredge small animals from the sea bottom. Some species eat only plankton, while others also catch fish.

Many toothed whales (Odontocetes) use their formidable batteries of teeth to catch and eat relatively large prey such as fish and mammals, sometimes even larger whales. Other toothed whales have developed specialized teeth, or even lost most of them, but still catch squid and fish. Recent genetic studies show that simple division into toothed and baleen whales does not fully reflect cetaceans' relationships. The largest toothed whale, the sperm whale, is actually a closer relative of baleen whales than of other toothed whales.

Senses in the sea

Lunge-feeding humpbacks emerge in a cloud of spray. (Folkens)

Whales are sensitive to sound; we have known this since whalers learned to approach them quietly. Yet the external ear opening is tiny—only a centimetre in the largest whales.

Researchers have recently paid much more attention to whale senses. Touch is important; whales respond to touching by other whales. Many captive whales—and some wild whales known as "friendlies"—seem to enjoy direct human contact. The few hairs of baleen whales, richly supplied with nerves, probably sense water movement.

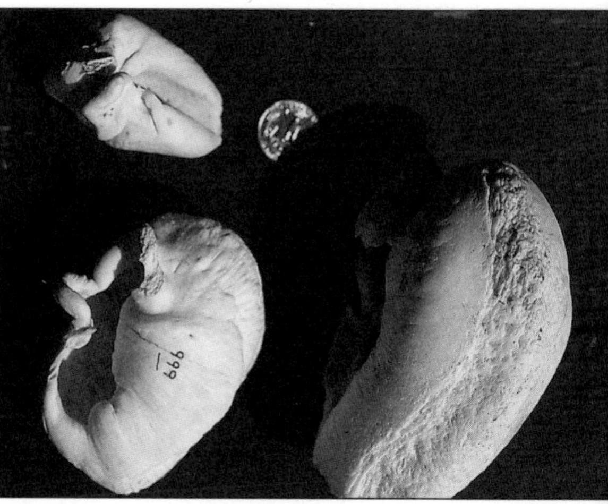

Fist-sized ear bones of baleen whales are solid bone. (DAES)

Taste seems to be limited, though dolphins will spit out putrid fish. Smell seems to have diminished as the breathing system changed. Toothed whales have no olfactory nerves, though baleen whales have some and can perhaps smell krill.

Underwater vision is possible only near the surface, as water absorbs much of the available light—four-fifths of it at a depth of 40 feet (10 m).

Paul Spong's experiments show that in both water and air an orca can see about as well as a cat. The spyhopping behaviour of several species suggests that aerial vision is useful.

Sea canaries and sonar

Though whalers termed belugas "sea canaries" for their musical calls, cetologists long failed to take seriously the sounds and hearing of whales. Why was whale hearing ignored for so long? As recently as 1953, in a book about his undersea adventures, *The Silent World*, Jacques Cousteau argued that existing recordings of underwater sounds had been greatly amplified. With the development of submarines during World War II, serious research—secret at first—began on ocean acoustics. As this work became public it became clear that the sea was a very noisy place indeed. Large aquaria initiated new research on smaller whales' sound production and hearing, and tested this fresh knowledge in the ocean. By 1986 Cousteau recognized that his once silent world "is a vast echo chamber and that its inhabitants are constantly bombarded with noise."

We now know that the acoustic centres of whales' brains and the associated auditory nerves, are proportionally larger than other

A humpback swimming in clear waters off Hawaii reminds us that a whale's eye view of the world is very different from ours. (Ellis/Ursus)

mammals'. Odontocetes in particular are sensitive to a huge range of sounds—from 100 to 150,000 Hz—compared with a human range of only 30 to 16,000 Hz. Many species of toothed whales not only hear nearby sounds but use a form of sound echolocation, better known as sonar. These species send out high-frequency sound pulses which are reflected back by solid objects. The whales can decode the returned reflections to obtain information about their surroundings. These sounds are not produced during emission of air (as when humans talk), but internally by air vibrating in the complex nasal passages. These noises are readily audible outside the whale's body, since water carries sound better than air. Some species focus echolocation sounds through the "melon," a bulbous part of the front of the skull containing oil, which serves as an acoustic lens. Hollow jawbones sense the returning sounds and transmit them to the ear.

Clicks produced by sperm whales have been recorded several miles away, and researchers have suggested that humpbacks' deepest sounds are audible more than 100 miles away, and fin whales' farther still—a distinct convenience to whales seeking others of their species.

Siren songs and haunted ships

Humans may have heard the humpback songs for centuries, for there are many stories of singing sirens and mermaids. Their calls led one crew of nineteenth-century whalers to desert a ship they believed was haunted. Humpback whales became famous as "singers," however, only when 1970s recordings revealed their varied vocal outputs. Recordings are also obtainable of other whales, including orcas, and some smaller dolphins and porpoises. The significance of these sounds has created much controversy. Some researchers consider them relatively unimportant; others, believing they approach the complexity of human language, have experimented with interspecies communication.

Humpback songs usually last six to thirty-five minutes, though one sang for twenty-four hours and was still at it when recording observers left. The songs form distinct syllables arranged in phrases and linked into themes. All humpbacks in a region sing the same "dialect" with individual variations, and the songs evolve through time. Only males in breeding grounds sing. This suggests whale song may have a similar function to birdsong in advertising the male's presence and perhaps defining a temporary territory.

John Ford at Blackfish Sound

John Ford was interested in whale acoustics from early in his career. Vancouver Aquarium Director Murray Newman invited him to the Arctic as an undergraduate in 1975 to study narwhal vocalizations. After a preliminary look at gray whales, he began a master's thesis in 1978 on orca sounds in Johnstone Strait, with the then revolutionary hypothesis that different pods had individual dialects.

John Ford at Telegraph Cove. (DAES)

With his little boat *Brown Bomber*, Ford and his wife Deborah established a camp on Parson Island, 12 miles (20 km) from Alert Bay. With a camera he helped sort out the northern pods, at the same time dangling a hydrophone overboard to record sounds made by the whales he photographed. Despite a few mishaps—such as an orca tipping the boat by taking hold of the microphone—he began to make sense of what he was hearing and seeing. Different pods each indeed had distinct sounds. They used clicks for echolocation of landmarks and prey, and used whistles and other calls to keep pod members in touch. Ford could eventually identify recorded pods by sound and returned to identify pods the navy had recorded twenty years earlier.

As Ford tried to record all the pods, his project grew into a PhD dissertation. Since finishing in 1984, he has extended his research to Alaskan orcas.

Four years later, Ford became curator of marine mammals

at the Vancouver Aquarium, where he occupies an office with a window on the whale pool. Here he found that captive whales from different regions could learn sounds from each other. The aquarium has published a collection of Ford's recordings, punningly titled *Blackfish Sound* after the area where he did much of his work.

Whale societies

The more we learn about whale societies the more complex and interesting they appear. When a whale gives birth, one or more other adult "midwives" often assist, helping the baby to surface for its first breath. A number of people have observed injured whales being supported by their fellows. Ancient stories of dolphins rescuing people were long dismissed as fables, but we now have so many records of dolphins of various species playing with people in the water, often picking them up and carrying them on their backs, that we know the stories probably contain some truth. A growing orca stays with its mother; indeed, the whole family group, for some or all of its life, is a strongly matriarchal society. By contrast, sperm whales seem to have a bull-and-harem social structure like land-based herding animals. Most intriguing is the discovery that sounds made by large rorquals carry for many miles. Since distant individuals can communicate and co-ordinate their actions, we can still regard them as members of one social group.

Underwater world

As we sail across the sea's temporary topography, we find it hard to know where we are unless we can sight land. We find it even harder to imagine the world that whales perceive. They live most of their lives under water, in a three-dimensional world with both an upper limit and a lower limit. Even so, whales do not live in a uniform water body, without landmarks and directions.

Close to land their habitat is bounded by islands and peninsulas that give an underwater shape to the water channels. Even out in the ocean the sea floor has true topography in the continental shelf, isolated islands and recently discovered midoceanic ridges. Whales may not dive to the ocean bottom, though some swim very deeply, but they may be aware of the depth below them. They must be sensitive to the complex of currents warm and cold, the upwellings of warmer water from deep in the ocean and warm

Cruise ship passengers on their way to Alaska often see whales along the dramatic Inside Passage. (DAES)

shallow breeding lagoons, the distribution of icebergs and pack ice, and streams of brackish water flowing from great rivers.

Occasionally whales turn up far from their usual haunts, since the ocean is a single body of water. In general, however, whales travel on relatively predictable paths, which once allowed whalers all too easily to find their prey. Some have definite migrations, moving from tropics to arctic seas in a regular cycle. Others return to breed in one place, as gray whales do in Mexico's Pacific coast lagoons. Whales with more limited territories, such as the resident orcas of Pacific Northwest waters, are surely aware of the local topography of channels and rubbing beaches.

Since many whales follow predictable paths, they must have some sort of guidance system. This may be as instinctive as the migration of birds that navigate by stars and the earth's magnetic field. We can reasonably suppose that whales have some memory and knowledge of this complex submarine geography, perhaps even of shore landmarks. Can we also imagine that one function of orcas' close social groups over long years is to permit older whales to teach younger whales their territorial landmarks and the location and timing of salmon runs?

Sometimes—in a puzzling, still inadequately explained phenomenon—whole pods of whales are stranded. Dead or dying whales are sometimes cast up on the shore, of course, often providing evidence of whales otherwise unknown in the area. But groups of perfectly healthy-seeming whales are sometimes cast up together, attracting much public attention. Volunteers often return smaller whales to the sea, only to see them strand themselves again.

Explanations include a parasite of the inner ear that confuses navigation, and the suggestion that whales may be sensitive to earth's fluctuating geomagnetic field; following its contours in migratory paths, occasionally they may become confused when these contours run from the sea onto the land.

Life on—and in—a whale

Whales themselves provide a home for a lot of life. Barnacles cover rough patches of skin on slower species such as humpbacks and right whales. Some barnacle species infest only one whale species, which implies that they spread by direct contact. They use the whale as a residence but feed on microscopic life in the adjacent water. Although the cumulative weight may slow down the whale, the barnacles may also be useful—humpbacks scar each other with barnacle-studded flippers in mating fights.

The outer skin of a gray whale is home to barnacles—some of which are found only on whales—and whale lice. (Dennis)

Among the barnacles, other crustaceans known as whale lice often live. These skeletal creatures, related to familiar sand hoppers, feed on the whale's peeling skin. Whales also have internal parasites including tapeworms which may grow to 50 feet (15 m) long.

A web of food

Ecologists construct diagrams called food webs to show the interrelationships of life forms and trace a community's energy flow from the simplest plants through grazers to mid- and high-level predators. Although we lack information to draw detailed food webs of undersea life, we can see where whales fit. The sea's basic food plants are usually small planktonic algae, eaten by everything from small planktonic animals to fish and squid. Some baleen whales live directly on planktonic animals. Many Odontocetes eat fish and squid, the mid-level ocean predators. Some orca groups sometimes attack other sea mammals, even other whales. Generally man—for once an accurate term, as few women have gone whaling—is the only predator of large whales. Living whales themselves are eaten by parasites, and dead whales by a multitude of scavengers from bacteria to bald eagles. Most return nutrients from decomposing whales to the sea, where other living creatures can use them.

Orcas and Dolphins

The Toothed Whales

Leaping Pacific white-sided dolphins.. (Morton)

WHICH MAMMAL HAS THE MOST TEETH? FEW PEOPLE WOULD suggest a dolphin, yet the tropical spinner dolphin averages 224 teeth and can have as many as 260, while the west's toothiest cetacean is the saddle-backed dolphin, averaging 200 teeth. (Primitive mammals have 44 teeth; most living groups have fewer.)

Whales also have bigger and longer teeth than any other mammals except elephants. The sperm whale's fist-sized teeth were the favourite medium for the whalers' art of scrimshaw, and the male narwhal's tusk—circulated in medieval Europe as the mythical unicorn's horn—can grow to 9 feet (2.7 m) long.

A friendly grin from Haida, long-time star of Sealand in Victoria's Oak Bay. (DAES)

The Odontocetes, or toothed whales, with 85 percent of living species, are the largest group of cetaceans. They use their teeth mainly to catch fast-moving prey such as fish and squid. With a few exceptions such as narwhals, teeth are not specialized for different tasks as in many land mammals. Young Odontocetes do not have a separate set of "milk teeth" as most mammals (including humans) do.

Scientists divide toothed whales into two major groups. The first includes fish-eating belugas, porpoises and dolphins. The second includes less familiar beaked whales and sperm whales, many of which pursue primarily squid. The sperm whale has teeth in the lower jaw but not in the upper. Only the males of the intriguing beaked whales have teeth, growing tusks from their lower jaws.

Toothed whales common in the Pacific Northwest include two members of the porpoise family (harbor and Dall's) and two of the dolphin family (the orca and Pacific white-sided dolphin). Several rarer dolphin species, several beaked whales and the sperm whale usually occur out to sea; we know them in coastal waters mainly from occasional strandings.

The orca, as the species most frequently seen on whale watching trips and most studied by scientists, appears first and in greatest detail in this chapter. Other frequently seen species follow in less detail. (For rarer species, see Chapter 5.)

Toothed whale checklist

These species occur on the west coast of North America. Underlined species, reasonably common in most of the area, appear in this chapter.

Family Monodontidae

Beluga *Delphinapterus leucas*

Family Phocoenidae

Dall's porpoise *Phocoenoides dalli*

Harbor porpoise *Phocoena phocoena*

Family Delphinidae

Rough-toothed dolphin *Steno bredanensis*

Pacific white-sided dolphin *Lagenorhynchus obliquidens*

Saddle-backed (common) dolphin *Delphinus delphis*

Bottlenose dolphin *Tursiops truncatus*

Striped dolphin *Stenella coeruleoalba*

Northern right whale dolphin *Lissodelphis borealis*

False killer whale *Pseudorca crassidens*

Orca (killer whale) *Orcinus orca*

Risso's dolphin *Grampus griseus*

Short-finned pilot whale *Globicephalus macrorhynchus*

Family Ziphiidae

Baird's beaked whale *Berardius bairdii*

Cuvier's beaked whale *Ziphius cavirostris*

Blainville's beaked whale *Mesoplodon densirostris*

Hector's beaked whale *Mesoplodon hectori*

Ginkgo-toothed whale *Mesoplodon ginkgodens*

Stejneger's beaked whale *Mesoplodon stejnegeri*

Hubbs' beaked whale *Mesoplodon carlhubbsi*

Family Kogiidae

Pygmy sperm whale *Kogia breviceps*

Dwarf sperm whale *Kogia simus*

Family Physeteridae

Sperm whale *Physeter catodon*

Orca—the largest dolphin

Public perceptions of the so-called killer whale have undergone radical transformation in recent years—and scientists have also learned many things that surprised them.

An orca breaches, leaping right out of the water. (Atleo)

The orca is one of the best known wild whales and the largest species often found in captivity. The species occurs more or less worldwide, apart from the high Arctic, and in summer sometimes visits north of the Bering Straits. It is particularly well known where large numbers live inshore, such as Puget Sound, around the San Juans and Gulf Islands, in the channels north of the Strait of Georgia and in Prince William Sound. Inland waters of British Columbia and Washington state have the world's densest orca populations. California has sightings both inshore and out to sea.

At around 27 feet (8 m) long, an adult male orca is an impressive sight; a large one may be over 30 feet (10 m) and weigh as much as 8 tons (7.2 tonnes). Its wedge-shaped dorsal fin alone can stand up some 6 feet (2 m). Young males resemble females, which are around 23 feet (7 m) when full grown and have a fin curving backward to a point. Resident orcas typically travel in a small pod of one or more adult males, several females of different ages and a calf or two. All members seem to be descendants of a single female, the pod's matriarch. Sometimes several pods combine into a superpod of as many as 80 or 100 orcas. Occasional lone orcas are usually adult males.

In Pacific Northwest waters, in good viewing conditions it is

Orcas travel in family groups called pods, typically combining adult males and females, and young of different ages. (Dennis)

hard to confuse orcas with any other species. Pod members surface more or less together, showing fins and then backs as they blow. They may gather in a group or travel together in short dives lasting up to half a minute followed by longer dives of up to four minutes. The white patch behind the eye is conspicuous from a distance, and at closer range, the paler saddle behind the dorsal fin shows clearly unless the whale is backlit. If an orca breaches or spyhops, its white underside is conspicuous. Females and young alone at a distance could resemble similar species such as the false killer whale or Risso's dolphin. Dall's porpoise has a similar pattern but is much smaller.

Orca facts

Size: males 27 to 32 feet (8 to 10 m)
Weight: males 8 tons (7.2 tonnes)
Description: striking black and white pattern, grayish saddle patch, dorsal fin up to 6 feet (2 m) in males
Reproduction: gestation around 12 months, calves 8 feet (2.4 m) at birth
Life span: 50 years or more
Food: fish or marine mammals
Distribution: inshore and offshore waters

Orca encounter

It was the sound we heard first—a long breathy "whoooff." We were enjoying a drink on our friend Harriet's living room deck at the end of an unusually hot May day. We all jumped up, raced to the deck rail and caught a glimpse of a long black body sinuously curving below the water surface very close to the shore. It was a big orca and it seemed to be moving in slow motion. As we waited to see if he would surface again, I noticed three triangular dorsal fins breaking the surface about half a mile offshore, so we knew a pod was coming through. Harriet gave a gasp and pointed, and coming around the point were three other orcas rolling and splashing. It looked for all the world as though they were playing. One of them came really close into the little bay, and as it expelled its breath it sounded as though it was right beside us, and we could see the fountain of water vapour.

The first orca surfaced several times as it swam past, and because of the height of the deck we could actually see its body below the water between breaths. Suddenly the view seemed full of orcas. Everywhere we looked there were small groups of shiny black sails. Then they put on a real show. One breached and water flew everywhere. A couple rolled on their sides and slapped the water with their flippers. We saw several flukes and one orca spyhopped right in front of us. There must have been over twenty of them, and we watched for fully fifteen minutes as they swam past. I think there was a school of fish coming through at the same time, as there was a raft of gulls around, but I don't know if the orcas were chasing fish or feeling playful after a good meal. —AJS

Spyhopping and lobtailing

Orcas are generally tolerant of human presence and may show a great variety of behaviour to lucky watchers. Pods may loaf around or be active travellers, swimming purposefully in a definite direction. They may spyhop (rise vertically from the water), or breach (leap from the water, often twisting in the air and landing on back or side). Other behaviours include lobtailing (splashing the surface with the tail) and porpoising (swimming rapidly while leaping like a porpoise). The most varied behaviour seems to occur when two pods meet and intermingle.

Although they usually swim near the surface, orcas are capable of deep dives; one off Alaska got tangled in a cable at 3,380 feet (1,030 m). Each pod travels actively most of the time and may move 100 miles (160 km) in a 24-hour period.

Most orcas simply disappear beneath the waters when they die, but occasionally dying or dead individuals are stranded. There have been only a few mass strandings in our area. A pod of eleven was reported near Masset in the Queen Charlotte Islands in January 1941, and there was a temporary stranding of an unknown number at Cherry Point on Vancouver Island in September 1944. In June 1945 twenty went aground near Estevan Point on the west coast of Vancouver Island. In March 1949 two males and one female orca swam a shallow stream into Von Donnop Lagoon on Cortes Island. There two baby whales were born; the younger male helped them to the surface. But the whales apparently could not find their way back out of the lagoon, and adults and babies all died.

Right: A row of spyhopping orcas may be trying to get a better view of their surroundings. (Morton R) Below: A baby orca resembles a small female, and often sticks close to its mother. (Morton)

Mating seems to take place primarily in the summer, but young orcas are born at any time of the year. About 8 feet (2.4 m) long, they are helped to the surface by another member of the pod and follow their mother (or another adult) closely for about six months. Existing information suggests that their life cycles are not too different from our own. The males grow their large dorsal fins between the ages of twelve and twenty; females bear young in the wild from about thirteen and may continue to give birth about every three years. Adults live at least forty or fifty years, probably longer. Resident pods remain together most of the time. Individuals that go missing never join other pods, so we usually assume that a whale not sighted for a year has died.

For years, the diet of the orca was dismissed with a few references to pods attacking large whales. The main evidence for its fierce disposition was a century-old European account of a single specimen whose stomach contained remains of thirteen porpoises and five seals; many people have assumed that these were all remains of one recent meal, instead of the accumulated indigestible remains of many. More recently, lengthy lists of recorded prey species have been compiled which, taken at face value, gave no hint that not all orcas ate the same prey.

In the early 1970s work by Michael Bigg, Paul Spong and others began to link much orca behaviour to movements of salmon in the Pacific Northwest. As this pattern became clearer, it became apparent that some orcas did not fit the killer whale image at all. Gradually a fascinating picture emerged of two apparently independent groups of orcas with significantly different appearance and vocalizations, distribution and behaviour patterns, preferred prey and feeding strategies. These have become known as residents and transients. More recently, researchers have identified a third group, the offshores.

Orcas or killer whales?

Known as the blackfish to West Coast fishermen and as the grampus in England, this species has long been called "killer whale" for its reputed ferocious attacks on warm-blooded prey. In recent years we have realized that this behaviour characterizes only some individuals and presents a misleading image of the overall species.

As long ago as 1874, whaler Charles Scammon used the term *orca*. This name comes from the not entirely clear scientific name, *Orcinus orca. Orcinus* has sinister overtones, as it may derive from *Orcus*, a Latin rendering for Phorcys, the Greek god of the underworld. *Orca* may have the same significance, in which case it is only subtly less negative than killer whale. Latin *orca* also means barrel, however, and may describe the species' rounded body. Although perhaps still not politically correct, at least this derivation carries fewer negative connotations than killer whale. Increasingly whale researchers use only "orca."

Residents eat fish

Our best known orcas are residents. They have more rounded dorsal fins and more variable saddle patches than transients, and are much more vocal, perhaps using sounds to co-ordinate pod movements.

The shape of a male orca's large dorsal fin often helps in positive identification of an individual. (Dennis)

Residents occupy mainly inside waters sheltered from the Pacific by Vancouver Island and the Olympic Peninsula, though they sometimes venture outside. Within these waters, distinct northern and southern groups roam, only occasionally invading each other's territory.

Southern residents are a single clan (J) of approximately 90 whales split into 3 pods (J1, K1 and L1). These occupy Puget Sound and the waters around the San Juans and Southern Gulf Islands.

From the northern end of the Strait of Georgia to Queen Charlotte Sound, the northern resident group comprises three clans (A, G and R), normally in 16 pods totalling about 200 individuals.

Residents feed almost exclusively on salmon and bottom fish, and their summer movements seem closely linked to those of their prey fish. (We don't know where they winter.) Seals and sea lions generally ignore residents, but occasionally—perhaps under stress from starvation—resident whales have attacked porpoises and seals. One intensive study turned up three records of such predation in 1976, 1977 and 1982. Recently—as fish stocks decline—there have been other reports. Three times since 1987, residents—L5 and her offspring—have been seen harassing and possibly devouring marine mammals.

Dylan: Portrait of a resident

Dylan belongs to L1, one of the three southern pods. The young bull was born in 1965, probably to Misky (L28), since he travelled close by her in his early years. Now that Dylan is older he is easy to spot. His tall skinny dorsal fin rises straight up on the back edge and has an obvious nick halfway down. His saddle patch is S-shaped on his left side.

Dylan lost his mother in summer 1994. Researchers photographed Misky on May 31, 1994 in an unusual place to see the pod; Johnstone Strait lies well beyond L1's northern range. Two days later the pod was seen rapidly travelling south near Nanaimo. The next day, in waters around the San Juan Islands, Misky was not with the pod. She has not been seen since and is presumed dead.

As they travel, Dylan now swims close to his young brother Mystery, born in 1991. Dylan's sister Sumner was born in 1984 but lived only a year. Although Dylan and Mystery are members of the large L1 pod, they often travel in a smaller subpod of approximately 14 members. This group is named the L12 subpod after its leader, a grandmother orca (L12) called Alexis. —AJS

Transients eat mammals

Transient groups travel through the same waters as residents but occur in smaller pods of generally less than six whales. Dorsal fins are generally pointed, and saddle patches are more uniformly gray than residents'. Transients more often travel in outside waters. Although transients occasionally take bottom fish, their food and feeding strategy differ from residents'. They are generally silent, perhaps listening for prey species. They cruise long distances, coming suddenly on marine mammal concentrations. Sometimes they hang around seal and sea lion haulouts and follow the rising tide as it floods haulout rocks, forcing seals to return to the water. A seal or porpoise may be attacked by the entire pod; members circle and take turns to strike with body, tail or fins. Stomachs of dead transients have been found to contain seal and sea lion remains and whale skin. They seem to travel much farther than residents; Washington and British Columbia transients have been identified as far north as Alaska and as far south as Monterey Bay, California.

Transient orcas kill and eat small mammals, like this Dall's porpoise. (Baird)

Clearly transients have given the orca its killer whale reputation—observer Rod Palm refers to them as the "motorcycle gang" of the killer whales. Until we understood transient feeding behaviour, all orcas were believed to eat species such as Dall's and harbor porpoises, white-sided dolphins, belugas, several baleen whale species, fur and harbor seals, Steller's sea lion and sea otters. Water birds recorded as prey—including auklets, cormorants, geese, grebes, guillemots, loons, murres and scoters—also probably reflect transient activities. Not even land mammals are safe. Palm reports, "In Alaska a pod of transients killed and ate a moose that was swimming across a channel." There are few documented reports of attacks on larger whales. One of the most striking is a May 1964 report from David Hancock, a naturalist, of an incident in which seven orcas caught and killed a Minke whale in Barkley Sound. The Minke was apparently in difficulty in shallow water and appeared to drown, as there was no blood in the water. The orcas ate the dorsal fin, tongue and flesh from the lower jaw and removed skin from the body.

Harbor seals are safe from transient orcas while they bask on the rocks, but are at risk as soon as they return to the water. (Dennis)

Orcas will attack gray whales (see Chapter 4). In Alaska, some 15 percent of humpbacks show orca tooth marks on flukes and flippers. Cynthia d'Vincent, a humpback researcher, reported two orca attacks on humpbacks. In one, a pod was attacking a bull Steller's sea lion when a young humpback swam through the commotion. The orcas changed target, charging the youngster repeatedly. Two adult humpbacks came in and flanked the young whale, slapping at the orcas with their flukes and rolling over to protect flukes and lips from attack.

No authentic report exists of orcas attacking humans, despite some highly coloured fiction and the possibility of this happening. In the Antarctic, orcas have bumped ice floes on which people were standing, using a known technique to knock seals into the water where the whales can attack them.

The mysterious offshores

In the late 1970s, researchers photographed large groups of orcas around the Queen Charlotte Islands but couldn't place them with other known groups. As the work of cataloguing residents and transients continued, excitement rose as it became clear that these orcas did not belong to either category.

Continuing observation of large groups, usually out to sea, has led to recent naming of a third group, the offshores. Dorsal fins are rounded, and saddle patches may be solid gray or open. Their food is not yet known, but they could be fish eaters; they are highly vocal like residents and would find it difficult to catch large concentrations of marine mammals. Occasional inshore sightings have been reported from Johnstone Strait, and a group of seventy-five was once observed off Victoria. The first specimen was found near Tofino in 1997.

Three groups—one species?

Although we now know the three main groups of orcas are distinct, only the resident pods are well known and many mysteries remain. For instance, we have constructed convincing genealogies for mother-child relationships, but we know almost nothing of the fathers and have rarely observed mating. Do orcas breed within the pod or with other pods? Residents, transients and offshores have visible differences—do these represent genetic distinctions or do the groups interbreed? If they are distinct, are the groups even part of the same species? In the Antarctic, Russian scientists identified distinctly different mammal-eating offshore orcas and fish-eating inshore orcas and attempted to name one as a separate species.

New research shows that the groups differ in their DNA; further study may lead to better understanding of the complex and fascinating orca.

Harbor porpoise

Once one of the most familiar cetaceans, the little harbor porpoise is mysteriously declining in numbers. In a 1948 study of Washington mammals it was "seen more often than any other cetacean in the state," but that is no longer true. The decline, not local but worldwide, is causing much alarm for the future of this species.

The harbor porpoise is the area's smallest cetacean, usually under five feet and 130 pounds (60 kg). Blunt-faced and thus a porpoise, this species is characterized by its size, dark back and low triangular dorsal fin. Its colour usually becomes paler on the sides and white on the belly, but patterns are not consistent. Porpoises may occur singly or in small groups, but occasionally as many as sixty individuals gather. Travelling harbor porpoises typically surface half a dozen times at roughly one-minute intervals.

The harbor porpoise occurs from California to north of the Aleutians, including Puget Sound and Juan de Fuca Strait. Large numbers winter in Prince William Sound, Alaska, which may be the most densely populated area. Groups of up to sixty gather north of the San Juans in summer and early fall; observation spots include Lime Kiln Park on San Juan Island and Washington Park on Fidalgo Island near Anacortes. Births usually take place from May to July. The harbor porpoise prefers shallow waters close to shore and sometimes even travels up rivers such as the Columbia.

Its main diet consists of squid and various fish; groups of porpoises will herd schooling fish. Nets set off the Olympic Peninsula, on the bottom in 40 to 44 fathoms or 240 to 264 feet (73.2 to 80.5 m), have caught and drowned harbor porpoises, which also eat bottom fish. A harbor porpoise was found dead near Ozette, Washington, having apparently choked on a 17-inch (44.5 cm) herring.

The boat-shy harbor porpoise does not ride bow waves and generally avoids would-be observers. It often travels alone or in small groups and rarely leaps out of the water. Although it suffers from trapping in offshore nets, pollution in inshore waters (particularly PCBs and DDT compounds) and possibly human disturbance, these problems alone may not explain the porpoise's decline.

Harbor porpoise facts

Size: 4.5 feet (1.4 m)
Weight: 90 lbs (41 kg)
Description: black above, shading to white beneath
Reproduction: gestation 10 to 11 months, calves 3 feet (1 m) at birth
Life span: 15 to 20 years
Food: small fish and squid
Distribution: coastal and sheltered inshore waters

Dall's porpoise

Dall's porpoise is the region's only common species that does not object to human company. It will bow-ride ahead of boats and does not always flee when approached, though its top speed of 30 knots makes it quite capable of keeping clear.

Similar in size to the harbor porpoise, Dall's porpoise is distinguished by its striking black and white appearance; it is sometimes reported as a "baby orca." Apart from the patch on its side, however, the Dall's pattern is different, with white on or near the tips of the dorsal fin and flukes. Another characteristic is the back's angle before the tail which led the Makah and Quileute First Nations of the west coast of Washington to call it "broken tail." The largest documented Dall's in the region was measured at 6.8 feet (2 m) and estimated to have weighed about 200 pounds (91 kg). Dall's porpoise is a steady swimmer, and when springing out of the water to breathe, creates a characteristic spray pattern called a rooster tail.

A Dall's porpoise shows its characteristic white dorsal fin. (Baird)

The porpoise is named for the American zoologist William Healey Dall (1845–1927). He sailed as quartermaster with Charles Scammon before undertaking independent survey work and collected the type specimen in the Aleutian Islands. (He is also remembered in the names of the Dall sheep and the Alaska blackfish, *Dallia pectoralis.*)

The Aleutians are an appropriate location for this north Pacific species, which ranges from the Bering Sea south to California and west to Japan. On the northwest coast it is often found in exposed seas such as the Gulf of Alaska and Strait of Juan de Fuca. It is common in Glacier Bay and Prince William Sound but is rarer in the Strait of Georgia, Puget Sound and other more southerly inland waters. Nevertheless, it can often be seen in Haro Strait, Admiralty Inlet and Saratoga Passage near Whidbey Island and from Lime Kiln Park on San Juan Island. The porpoise travels California inshore waters in winter.

Small groups of up to 15 in the southern range join into larger groups between 30 and 100 individuals in spring and fall on the Washington and British Columbia coasts, and as many as 200 in Alaska. In spring 1980 a US fishery research ship reported a group of some 3,000 porpoises moving north through Stephens Passage in southeastern Alaska. Observations suggest calving both in February to March and again in July to August.

Dall's porpoise has been recorded eating squid, hake and lantern fish. Some of its prey species live more than 3,000 feet below the surface, but perhaps rise to shallower waters at night. The north Pacific population in 1986 was estimated at 920,000, but Japanese drift nets set in the Gulf of Alaska are known to drown 50,000 to 100,000 porpoises, many of them pregnant females, each year. After tests of the damage off Vancouver Island in 1986 and 1987, drift nets were forbidden in Canadian waters. Although international efforts have been made to outlaw them, there is little doubt they are still being used.

Studies of Dall's porpoises have begun around Whidbey Island, Washington state and Haro Strait between Canada and the USA. Researchers can identify individual Dall's porpoises by white patches on fin and flukes. Preliminary results suggest that the animals live in the area year-round.

Dall's porpoise facts

Size: males 6 to 7.5 feet (1.8 to 2.4 m)
Weight: 270 lbs (123 kg)
Description: black, with white patch below and on dorsal fin and tail
Reproduction: gestation 10 to 11 months, calves 3.5 feet (1 m) at birth
Food: fish and squid
Distribution: offshore, coastal and partly sheltered waters

Pacific white-sided dolphin

A group of white-sided dolphins defines the term *joie de vivre*, for they are among the liveliest of the small whales. They make repeated, apparently effortless leaps, porpoise around like aquatic dogs and drive the shutterbug to distraction by appearing wherever they are least expected. It is hard to imagine they are not waiting for applause. On one occasion, a Pacific white-sided dolphin breached with such enthusiasm that it ended up on the deck of a research vessel, 10 feet out of the sea. Fortunately the amused crew quickly returned it to its element.

You can probably recognize a Pacific white-sided dolphin from its behaviour before you get close enough to find field marks. Up close, you may have the chance to study a small group frolicking by your boat or riding a bow wave. It has the dark beak of a dolphin, and the species' characteristic white stripes on the sides and two-coloured, sharply curved dorsal fin. Both English and scientific

Pacific white-sided dolphins leap energetically, so they can often be identified at a distance. (Baird)

names are so long that whale watching folk often nickname this lively dolphin "lag," a shortening of its scientific name. Look for this dolphin anywhere in north Pacific waters from the Aleutians southward, especially in summer. Some dolphins remain in inside waters year-round; in fall and winter greater numbers gather there. Hecate Strait and the Straits of Georgia and Juan de Fuca all provide regular sightings. Schools may be small, but one group of 1,000 was sighted 25 miles (40 km) off the Queen Charlotte Islands in June 1959, and even larger groups have been recorded. Small pods may be seen off the California coast at any time, though numbers increase in winter. Recent estimates of the north Pacific population are 30,000 to 50,000. White-sideds eat squid and smaller fish, including anchovies and hake.

A partial skull from a midden near Port Hardy suggests that First Peoples in the past ate dolphins.

Pacific white-sided dolphin facts

Size: 7 to 8 feet (2.1 to 2.4 m)
Weight: 200 to 300 lbs (90 to 140 kg)
Description: black, gray and white dazzle pattern, short beaks, curved dorsal fin
Reproduction: gestation 9 months, calves 3 feet (1 m) at birth
Food: squid and fish
Distribution: coastal and larger sheltered waters

Grays, Humpbacks and Minkes

The Baleen Whales

A gray whale spyhops to take a look around. (Folkens)

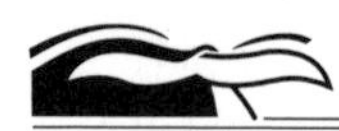

ANYONE WITH A FRIENDLY DOG OR CAT PROBABLY KNOWS OF THE hard ridges across the roof of its mouth. These are made of keratin, similar to the material of our fingernails. Imagine a dog enlarged a hundred times, without teeth but with these ridges extended into long fringed plates; now you can visualize the mouth of a baleen whale.

Over millions of years baleen whales—classed as Mysticetes after the Greek for "moustached whales"—gradually depended less on their teeth and developed new feeding strategies using multiple banks of baleen as filters. As many as 400 baleen plates, each a quarter inch (0.6 cm) thick, line each side of the whale's mouth. Each plate is a long triangle of horny, flexible keratin, fringed with coarse fibres on the inner side. The longest baleen belongs to the bowhead (an arctic species mentioned only briefly in this book), whose plates can stretch 15 feet (4.5 m) long and must be folded back for the whale to close its mouth.

Baleen whales feed by opening the mouth, ingesting water filled with plankton and small fish, then expelling the water, leaving plankton caught on the fibrous edges of the baleen plates. This is then scraped off by the tongue and swallowed.

The baleen whales have a double blowhole, unlike the toothed whales, which have a single blowhole. Many Mysticetes also have grooves on the throat, allowing them to expand their size even more when feeding.

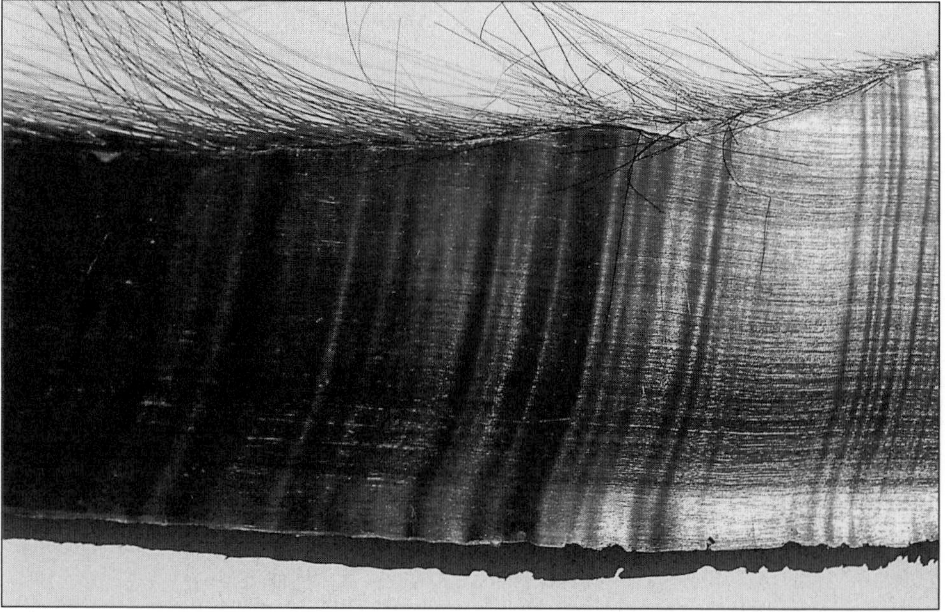

Baleen plates edged with fringes allow mysticetes (baleen whales) to sweep plankton out of the ocean. (DAES)

The blue whale, like other baleen whales, has a double blowhole. (Folkens)

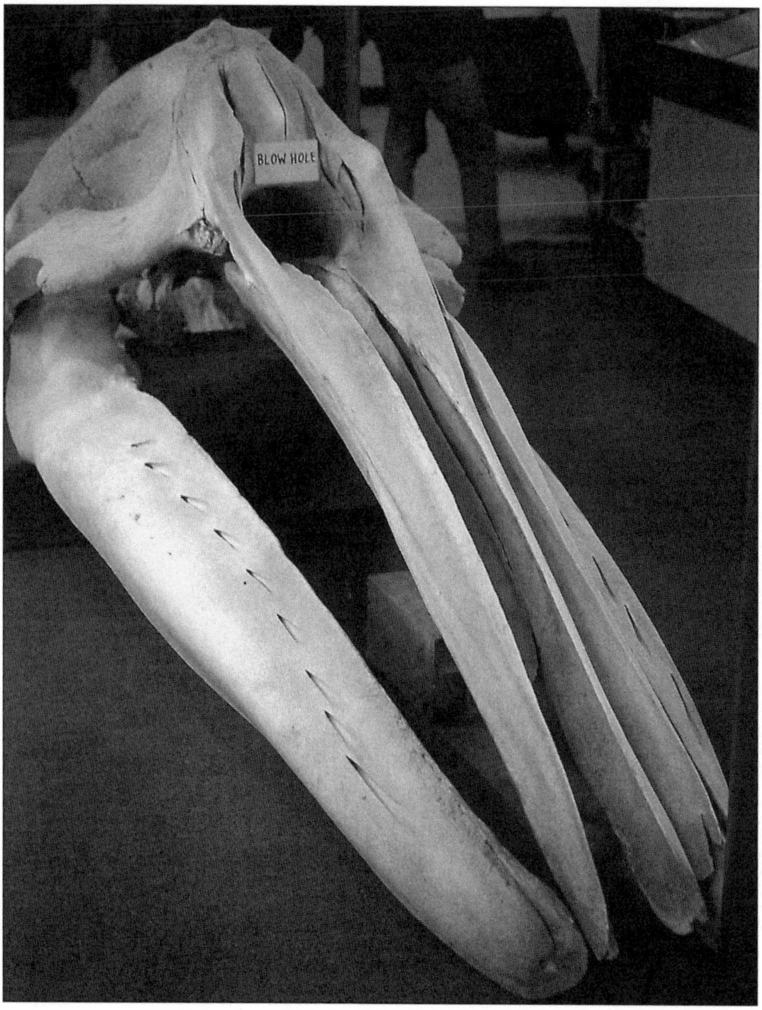

A gray whale skull on exhibit in Tofino shows the jawbones that support plates of baleen. (DAES)

There are three families of Mysticetes. Right whales are slow-moving plankton eaters with no grooves in their throats. The few species include the northern right whale from our area, its relative the southern right whale from the Antarctic and the bowhead from the high Arctic. The gray whale is the most abundant baleen whale in our region. Classified in its own family, it has two or four throat grooves. Although some cetologists consider it the most primitive baleen whale, others are unconvinced; they point out that its fossils are all of recent date. Members of the largest Mysticete family are known as "rorquals" from the Norwegian name *rorhval*, meaning "whale with pleats," for the fin whale. All rorquals have expandable grooves in the underside of the throat and—unlike other Mysticetes—a dorsal fin. The humpback is often visible in the Gulf of Alaska; the Minke frequents the Strait of Juan de Fuca and other inland waters. (For the rarer rorquals, see Chapter 5.)

Baleen whale checklist

Baleen whale species reasonably common in the Pacific Northwest (underlined) appear in this chapter.

Family Balaenidae

Northern right whale *Balaena glacialis*

Family Eschrichtiidae

<u>Gray whale</u> *Eschrichtius robustus*

Family Balaenopteridae (Rorquals)

<u>Humpback whale</u> *Megaptera novaeangliae*
Blue whale *Balaenoptera musculus*
Fin whale *Balaenoptera physalus*
Sei whale *Balaenoptera borealis*
Bryde's whale *Balaenoptera edeni*
<u>Minke whale</u> *Balaenoptera acutorostrata*

The resilient gray whale

Several species have returned from near extinction, but few have done so twice. Gray whales, vulnerable because they breed in a few places accessible to whalers, have triumphed over two waves of exploitation—around the 1860s and 1920s—and successfully recovered their numbers.

Along much of their migration route—one of the longest of any mammal—grays now attract huge numbers of whale watchers and

A gray whale spout is often the first sign that whales are in the area. (Maloff)

support a multimillion-dollar tourist business. This population of the gray whale is the only one with a future; its west Pacific relatives are seriously threatened, and former populations on both sides of the Atlantic are long extinct.

The gray whale was first described scientifically when a fossil skeleton was excavated in Sweden in 1859. Seven years later the American palaeontologist and zoologist Edward Drinker Cope described a specimen taken from the Pacific fishery. The Atlantic gray whale seems to have been the large whale that Norwegians hunted in the ninth century; it was recorded from Iceland in the seventeenth century and New England in the eighteenth. The gray, apparently one of the first casualties of whaling, disappeared before it was properly documented.

Gray whale facts

Size: 35 to 50 feet (10 to 15 m)
Weight: 20 to 40 tons (18 to 36 tonnes)
Description: gray, mottled white with barnacles, no dorsal fin but several prominent bumps on back
Baleen: 160 to 180 plates, each 16 to 20 inches (40 to 51 cm) long
Reproduction: gestation around 12 months, calves 15 feet (4.5 m) at birth
Life span: average 30 to 40 years, up to 60
Food: mainly amphipod crustaceans
Distribution: coastal from Baja California to north of Bering Straits

The scientific name Cope used for this species translates as "the gray swimmer along rocky shores," an accurate description of

the appearance and habitat of the Pacific population.

When its back heaves above the water, its skin appears dull charcoal gray. On the move, it will typically blow its heart-shaped spout between three and five times at intervals of ten to twenty seconds. After renewing its air supply, it is likely to dive for three to seven minutes. The gray has no dorsal fin, but a close view shows the spine's half-dozen knobby ridges that make the species easy to recognize. Whitish patches on the head, back, flukes and flippers are hitchhiking barnacles, which grow on the whale and shelter a variety of fellow travellers.

Gray whale encounter

The day was not auspicious; it was cold, wet and windy with a choppy sea, a challenge to the strongest sea legs. Amazingly, a boatload of keen whale watchers turned up at the Tofino dock and off we went. We bobbed around for ages. Visibility was poor and the day so gray that it was hard to tell sea from mist from sky. I spotted several spouts in the distance, but the whales had more sense than us; they weren't spending much time on the surface. The wind was cold, the sea grew rougher and we were almost ready to give up.

Grays sometimes come into sheltered waters, attracting whale watchers near Sidney on Vancouver Island. (Maloff)

Suddenly I gave a shout. I'd caught sight of a spout from the corner of my eye, about 100 yards off the left side of the boat. I leaned over and gazed intently ahead of it, hoping to guess where the whale would surface again. I was glad I was looking in the right spot or I would have missed it. There was just a glimpse of a long curving back slowly arching through the waves, barely breaking the surface. I was astonished. The curve of the spine was enormous; it went on forever. It was so knobby you could almost see the giant vertebrae under the glistening skin. But most astonishing of all, the gray whale wasn't gray! It was a steely gray-blue with deep purple and bright orange splotches on it, rather like lichen on a rock. I found out afterward that the splotches of colour were patches of barnacles and sea lice that hitch a ride on these gigantic mammals.

The whale must have known our boat was there, but it didn't react in any way to our presence. It went on its way; obviously humans did not compute in its scheme of things, and it wasn't going to interrupt its marathon migration to interact with us. This made me feel small and inadequate. There we were, a pinpoint bobbing around on the surface of this massive underwater world we could never be part of. I realized how little I knew about these leviathans and their reality.

I saw the whale for only a few seconds but that glimpse of the gigantic, mysterious and elusive gray whale was one of the most impressive sights of my life. —AJS

Barnacles and whale lice

The gray whale provides a home for a barnacle, *Cryptolepas rhachianecti*, not found on any other whale species. The free-swimming larva finds a place—usually on the head, back, flukes or flippers—and burrows into the skin. Then it grows a protective shell (barnacles are related to crabs) and kicks floating food particles into its mouth with its jointed legs. It uses the whale only as transport to fresh food supplies. Although barnacles doubtless irritate the whale, they are otherwise harmless, unlike the three species of whale lice that shelter among their shells and gather in folds in the whale's skin. Whale lice are amphipod crustaceans about half an inch (1.3 cm) in diameter; they look like flattened crabs with segmented bodies. One whale louse, *Cyamus ceti*, also infests other kinds of whales; the other two whale lice, *Cyamus scammoni* and *Cyamus kessleri*, only infest the gray whale. The lice feed actively on the whale's skin and gather around injured areas. Barnacles and whale lice together must give the whales more than a few itches that they can't easily scratch. Joe Garner, a Salt Spring resident, remembers gray whales rubbing on island rocks many years ago. Such behaviour does not seem common in this region, but Russians have recorded gray whales rubbing on pebble beaches in Siberia, leaving behind a litter of barnacle fragments to show the effectiveness of the technique.

A close encounter with a friendly gray whale off Vancouver Island. (Dennis)

The gray gourmand

Some whalers called this species the "mussel digger," misunderstanding the whale's choice of food but noting its unusual feeding strategy. The gray is the only whale that regularly feeds by "vacuum cleaning" the sea floor. Grays feed mainly in the northern part of their range, along the shallow continental shelf, usually 165 to 225 feet (50 to 69 m) deep, but they may also feed in water as shallow as 15 feet or as deep as 330 feet (4 to 100 m). Bottom sand and mud is generally rich in small animals, particularly amphipods under an inch (2.5 cm). These are related to the sandhoppers familiar to beach visitors and to lice that live on whales' bodies. Some amphipods form dense mats of tubes which cover the sea floor, while others live solo lives in the surrounding muck. At its richest, the bottom muck may contain as many as 3,000 amphipods per square foot (32,600 per m^2), providing up to 90 percent of the whales' food.

Hungry grays dive to the bottom for as long as twenty minutes. They turn on their sides and swim along the sea floor, churning up bottom sediments with their snouts,

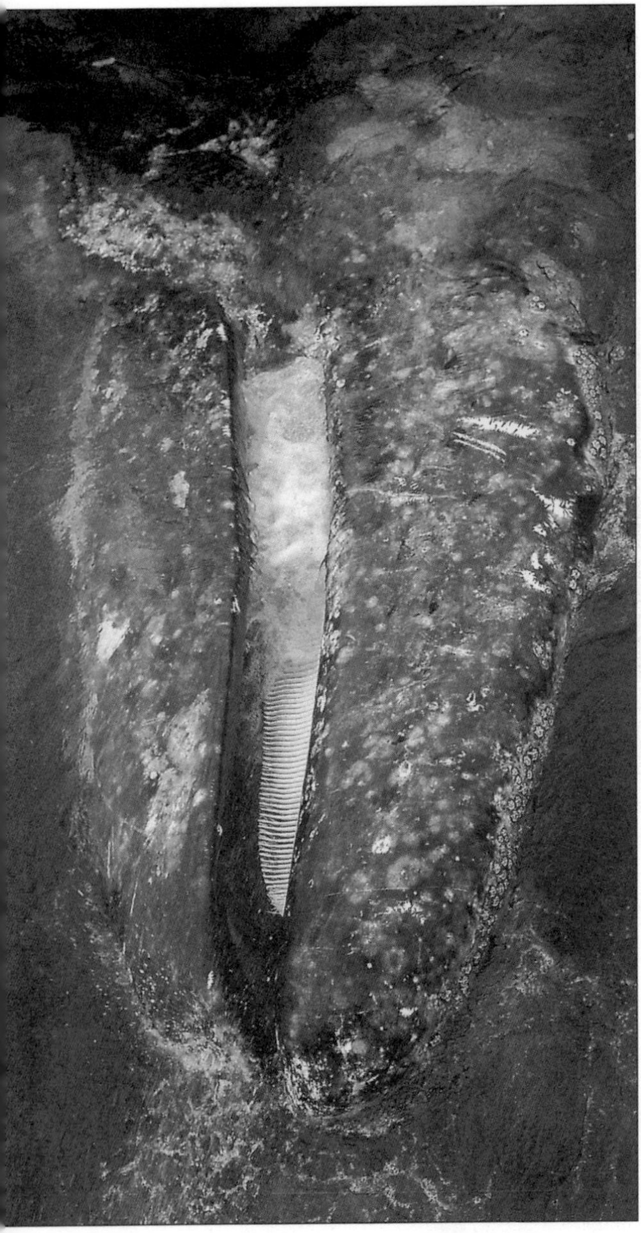

A feeding gray whale squeezes water through its baleen. (Folkens)

and sucking in the mud and its organisms by retracting their tongues. The whales catch the amphipods on the baleen on the opposite side of their mouths and lick them back to the gullet. Most grays are "right mouthed," preferring to scrape their right side along the sea floor, as the lack of barnacles and worn baleen on that side indicates. As with humans, a few individuals are more comfortable using the other side.

During the five-month summer eating binge, individual whales eat about 67 tons (60 tonnes) of food. They are clearly interested in quantity rather than quality—gourmands rather than gourmets.

Although whalers saw plumes of mud thrown up by grays feeding in clear water, only relatively recently was this behaviour successfully filmed at Pachena Bay near Bamfield on the west coast of Vancouver Island. Grays also swim through schools of small fish, presumably using the tactics of other baleen whales; having only two to four grooves in the underside of the throat, however, they cannot expand their mouths as fully. One individual around Gray's Harbor, Washington, had many rainbow smelt in its gullet. Grays sometimes take kelp into their mouths, probably not eating plants but simply sucking small creatures off the kelp.

Plankton and predators

Gray whales disturb more sea floor life than they eat, and plumes of mud in the water may attract birds such as phalaropes and auks, which pick up leftover tidbits. Their browsing leaves large areas of the sea floor covered with rectangular pits that one researcher compared to a battlefield in an old John Wayne movie. This disturbance spreads fine silts, which might otherwise bury bottom-dwelling life, and stirs up nutrients which encourage the growth of plankton. This in turn stimulates the growth of fish and other whale species that feed directly or indirectly on planktonic plants and animals. It is possible that devastated sea floor areas are seeded with young amphipods and soon recover their productivity.

Orcas attacking gray whales

Gray whales have few enemies other than whalers but are occasionally attacked by transient orcas; many carry tooth scars on their flippers and flukes, though there are few well-documented accounts of such attacks. Charles Scammon, a whaler, watched three orcas attack a gray cow and her calf in a California lagoon in 1858. Although the calf was already three times the size of an orca they "made alternate attacks upon the old whale and her offspring, finally killing the latter, which sunk to the bottom...During the struggle, the mother became exhausted, having received several deep wounds about the throat and lips." After the young one died, the orcas started to feed from it; the mother made her escape "leaving a track of gory water behind." Scammon considered that orcas rarely attacked adult whales, but preyed "with great rapacity on their young." He did report orca attacks on whale carcasses already killed by whalers and tied fast to their ship.

Few other attacks have been documented in more than a century since Scammon's book was published, though in the late 1960s an orca group off California harassed gray whales and once killed and partly ate a calf. Although gray whales and transient orcas often appear near each other off Clayoquot, there have been few British Columbia observations of species interactions. Florence Tickner reported an undated incident near Hope Island. A Langara lightkeeper reported several orcas attacking two gray whales on September 10, 1960. The best documented record comes from Rod Palm, Earl Thomas and John Ford, who were all in separate boats off Tofino on April 22, 1994. Rod observed a group of five orcas identified as the U1 transient pod (nicknamed Motley Crew). Earl later saw the orcas, as did a gray whale. It changed course and came within 33 feet (10 m) of his boat, when he saw it was accompanied by a calf. The orcas split to flank the gray, which picked up the calf in one of its flukes and rolled onto its back. The male orca several times "raised his head, with mouth agape, up onto the side of the mother in an apparent attempt to get the calf." The orca failed, however. The gray righted itself and dived with the calf, and was then left alone. John Ford later observed the orca pod heading away. Apparent attacks do not always seem to be serious—one observer in Alaska recorded a pack of orcas sliding up and over the back of an apparently unconcerned female gray whale for half an hour. Grays do not provide significant amounts of food for animals other than orcas until they die, when a carcass cast ashore can create a feast for millions of bacteria and flocks of scavenging bald eagles.

Long migration

The gray whale has become well known because a large part of the course of its long migration—about 5,000 miles (8,000 km) in each direction—is along populated shores. This remarkable journey takes it through waters ranging between 5° and 22° Celsius (41° to 72° F). The only mammal migrations of comparable length are those of other large whales, such as the humpback population that travels between the Antarctic and Australia.

They begin leaving the Mexican breeding grounds in February and travel north past California. First come the adult cows, then

Grays migrate along the west coast in small groups. (Dorst)

the bulls and immatures, and last the mothers with new calves. The whales are lean, having eaten little in the south, but still average 50 miles (80 km) each day. The Pacific Northwest states and British Columbia see the whales from February onward as they migrate north close to the rocky shores. Most pass Oregon during mid-March to mid-May. They pass Washington until late May, when the last migrating animals leave the Olympic Peninsula. They migrate west of Vancouver Island between February and June, then pass the Queen Charlottes and cross the Gulf of Alaska. Most funnel through Unimak Pass in the Aleutians into the Bering Sea between April and June.

From Oregon northward, a few drop out of the migration and linger throughout the summer. Individuals often remain off Westport, Washington. Up to fifty grays sometimes appear off Long Beach on Vancouver Island through the summer, where researchers have noted some individuals returning several years in succession.

We have no clear understanding of how migrating whales find their way, but movement close to the coast may give them more clues than offshore travel. Whales may hear the sound of surf and perhaps the snapping of bottom-dwelling shrimps, while primitive sonar may help them detect shallow water—they travel mainly through water less than 30 fathoms or 180 feet (54.9 m) deep. It is possible that they are sensitive to changes in water smell or taste as they cross river outflows, and it has been suggested that the whales can navigate by the earth's magnetic field as birds do.

During the five-month summer, grays feed voraciously on the rich sediments of the shallow Arctic and Pacific sea bottoms. Here they recoup their fat supplies, gaining as much as 16 to 30 percent of their body weight and putting on 6 inches (15 cm) of blubber.

The southward migration begins in fall, with most of the population passing Unimak Pass during October to December. Pregnant females lead, followed by bulls and finally cows still accompanied by young calves. They cross the Gulf of Alaska at about 115 miles (185 km) a day and travel south farther offshore than in spring, reaching the Washington coast (usually in rainy weather) from late October to mid-December. They pass the Oregon and California coasts from late November to Christmas and New Year on their way to their breeding grounds in Baja California. The fall migration from Unimak Pass to Baja California normally takes about 55 days, but individuals may linger on the north coasts as late as December and January.

A spyhopping gray--perhaps it is watching the whale watchers. (Baird)

Togetherness

Along Baja California the gray whales congregate in a few breeding lagoons. Here the adult whales (sexually mature at five to eleven years) mingle and mate for several weeks. Each encounter is a leisurely process in which two or more males keep company with one female for hours on end. Sometimes the short-flippered gray male seems to have trouble staying close enough to the female to allow breeding, and there are reports that males take turns to support her while she is copulating with another male.

A female calves in the lagoons after a year's migration, producing a 1-ton (0.9 tonne) calf and helping it to the surface on her own to take its first breath. Her milk contains 55 percent fat, so the calf grows rapidly.

Charles Scammon, US whaler and scientist

Charles Melville Scammon was born in Maine on May 28, 1825. By 1850 he had made his way to California and by 1852 was skipper of the brig *Mary Helen*, outward bound to hunt seals, sea elephants and whales off Mexico. In the next decade or so, as a whaler and revenue captain, he travelled the Pacific coast from Peru to Siberia and took a keen interest in whales and other marine animals.

He made his most famous discovery in 1855 when he entered the Baja California lagoon Ojo de Liebre, later known as Scammon's Lagoon. He was the first to find a gray whale breeding ground and thus precipitated its first plunge toward extinction; he and other whalers spared neither cows nor calves in their frantic pursuit of profit.

No ordinary whaler, Scammon had aspirations as a zoologist. In the Strait of Juan de Fuca in October 1870, he documented a whale that seemed to be a new species and in 1872 described it as the Davidson piked whale, *Balaenoptera davidsoni* (now not considered distinct from the Minke). Probably the same year he met the celebrated zoologist Louis Agassiz, to whom he later dedicated his book *Marine Mammals of the Northwestern Coast of North America, Together with an Account of the American Whale Fishery.* This remarkable book, written with the help of two zoologists—Edward Cope, a describer of the gray whale, and William Dall, for whom Dall's porpoise is named—documents many whale observations and hunting experiences by Scammon and other whale captains.

Scammon retired in 1895 and died in 1911. His book sold poorly and most copies burned in the San Francisco fire. It was reprinted almost a century after its first appearance, however, and without it we would know much less of the earlier history of West Coast marine mammals.

Fluctuating populations

The disappearance of the gray whale from both sides of the Atlantic shows the vulnerability of a species with a predictable migration close to shore. Although the First Nations hunted the Pacific gray, there is no evidence that they had serious impact on its numbers. Only when whaling ships arrived from the Atlantic did the population begin to decline.

Estimates of the 1850s northwestern gray whale population run as high as 25,000, but after discovery of the breeding lagoons the population dropped to 4,000 in the mid-1870s. From 1905 modern whaling stations operated on the West Coast; by 1914 factory ships had arrived, and by mid-century the gray whale population fell to about 250. The first International Convention for the Regulation of Whaling, signed in 1946, prohibited the killing of gray whales except by aboriginal peoples and by governments for aboriginal use. With this protection, the whale has again made a remarkable comeback, and the population has been estimated as high as 25,000. Grays are beginning to return to once abandoned inshore waters.

The returning humpback

A century ago, people might see humpbacks anywhere in the protected waters of Washington state and British Columbia. A short period of whaling soon cleared out the small population, but it took some effort—in 1895 an old bull harpooned in Henderson

An Alaska humpback waves his flukes as he dives. (Folkens)

Bay near Puget Sound towed the small boat for "five long days and nights" before it was killed. Humpbacks on the continental shelf have sustained longer active whaling and still survive in numbers off southeastern Alaska, where watchers consistently see them. Now that the species is protected, individuals are creeping back into their former haunts in the Strait of Juan de Fuca, and more are seen every year off the west coast of Vancouver Island.

Humpback whale facts

Size: 48 to 58 feet (14 to 18 m)
Weight: 34 to 45 tons (31 to 41 tonnes)
Description: large head with tubercles; black body, white below, small dorsal fin, large flippers
Baleen: 270 to 400 plates, up to 25 inches (65 cm) long
Reproduction: gestation 11 to 12 months, calves 14 feet (4 m) at birth
Food: krill and fish
Distribution: Bering Sea and south

The humpback blows a low bushy spray and typically breathes at the surface for two or three minutes before sounding for a long period. Before sounding, it flings its flukes into the air in a characteristic way, showing the patterns of white marks underneath the tail that permit identification of individual whales. It is hard to mistake a humpback in a playful mood for any other whale. The big barrel body, tubercled head and long flippers that sometimes wave above the water are all characteristic.

From about May, humpbacks appear in near-shore continental shelf waters from north of the Aleutians south to California. Particular areas of concentration include the eastern Aleutians (particularly Unimak Pass), Prince William Sound, Glacier Bay, Stephens Passage, Frederick Sound and the Alexander Archipelago waterways. Wintering humpbacks cluster in two areas: about 500 gather around Hawaii, and another 100 gather on the Pacific coast between Vancouver Island and California. Both groups of wintering animals may be of the same stock.

Since the 1970s, humpbacks have slowly returned to the more southerly inland waters where they were once common. In July and August, groups of around five feed on Juan de Fuca Bank and La Perouse Bank, up to 40 miles (64 km) off Vancouver Island and the Olympic Peninsula. Small numbers were seen near Whidbey Island in 1976 and 1978, and in 1986 a single animal travelled for six days from Tacoma into Saanich Inlet.

A humpback catches a lot of its food by lunge feeding, thrusting suddenly forward into a school of fish or concentration of plankton. (Baird)

Lunge feeding and bubble nets

Humpbacks feed on both planktonic crustaceans and the schools of small fish that the plankton attracts. Humpbacks use the lunge feeding technique of most other baleen whales, approaching and swimming rapidly through concentrations of food with their great mouths open and licking the food off the baleen with their tongues. Many observed groups have developed their own techniques, however. One remarkable method is best known from Alaska.

The whales use bubble net feeding to hunt both plankton and fish. A group of one to eight whales swims upward in a spiral from around 50 feet (15 m) below a concentration of food, releasing a stream of bubbles from their blowholes. When the prey moves away from the ring of disturbed water and up toward the surface, the open-mouthed whales rise to feed on the concentrated food supply. They usually act co-operatively, but on one occasion two humpbacks made a net only to have two others crash the party and take the prey.

Bubble feeding was first observed by Norwegian whaler A. Ingebrigsten in the Arctic Ocean in 1929 and has since occasionally been observed in the Atlantic. It was not until 1968 that Charles and Virginia Jurasz made similar observations in southeast Alaskan waters. The technique has since been observed with some regularity; in 1978 a National Geographic crew filmed it and it appears in their splendid IMAX movie.

Songs and cycles

Sometimes co-operating whales sing during bubble net feeding. We don't know whether this is intended to scare the fish or to coordinate activity, but in its winter range the humpback has become the most famous cetacean singer.

North Pacific humpbacks become adult between the ages of six and twelve years. Breeding takes place in the wintering grounds; in the warm, clear waters off Hawaii humpback mating behaviour is increasingly well known. Between October and March, courting whales indulge in much racing, breaching and splashing. Calves nurse for about a year, becoming independent when they reach about 26 feet (8 m).

A century ago the north Pacific population was an estimated 15,000, but between 1905 and 1929 whaling killed at least 18,000. The humpback has been fully protected in the north Pacific since 1965. Current estimates suggest that there are only about 6,000 humpbacks worldwide, of which between one and two thousand live in the north Pacific.

The inconspicuous Minke

The Minke whale (pronounced "minky") reputedly got its odd name after a Norwegian whale gunner mistook one for a much larger blue whale. His fellow whalers thought this so funny that they jokingly named the small whales after him.

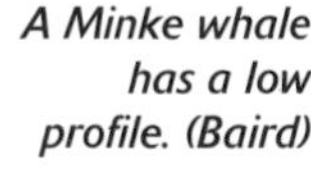

A Minke whale has a low profile. (Baird)

Minkes are the smallest baleen whales found in our region, and though local individuals are usually smaller, elsewhere they can grow to a respectable 30 feet (10 m). Nevertheless, Minkes can be difficult to locate.

Minke facts

Size: 26 to 30 feet (8 to 9 m)
Weight: 6 to 8 tons (5 to 7 tonnes)
Description: smallest rorqual; small dorsal fin far back, dark gray above, lighter below
Baleen: 260 to 360 plates, largest 12 inches (30 cm) long
Reproduction: gestation 10 to 11 months, calves 10 feet (3 m) at birth
Food: fish and squid
Distribution: Northeast Pacific, inshore and offshore waters

Their blow is more often heard than seen. When they are loafing or travelling, their small size and small, sharply curved dorsal fin are the most obvious clues. Only when feeding are Minkes more vigorously active. Then a sharply pointed head may be visible, or a close view could show a distinctive white band on a pectoral fin. In the open ocean Minkes can be hard to distinguish from the young of larger species, but in Puget Sound they are usually the only baleen whales to be seen.

Quasimodo in the San Juans

Individual names are often given to particular identifiable whales. Bubbles and Captain Hook, Quasimodo and Jackie O, Helter and Skelter are nicknames of the more than twenty Minke whales which have been observed in Puget Sound. As for orcas, illustrations of Minke fin patterns have been published to help local travellers recognize individuals and report their movements. In the summer, these whales maintain individual territories that do not seem to overlap. Summering Minkes may also be found as far north as Alaska, the Bering Sea and beyond. In the winter they migrate up to 6,000 miles (9,000 km), as far south as California or the equator.

In the San Juans, Minkes appear regularly at Hein Bank and Salmon Bank, in San Juan Channel and southwest of Sandy Point on Waldron Island. Farther north, they frequent the straits south and east of the Southern Gulf Islands, including the Strait of Georgia. Out in the ocean they live on fish, including saffron cod and anchovy, but in sheltered waters they feed on small fish such as herring and sand lance. Individual whales specialize in different feeding methods. Some approach a shoal from below, lunging out of the water with an open mouth and extended throat. Others wait

A breaching Minke whale is an unusual sight. (Pitman)

until larger fish gather in concentration at the surface, attracting flocks of birds, and emerge unexpectedly in the middle, scaring the birds away.

Although relatively small, Minkes have few enemies. Attacks by orcas, presumably transients, have been documented. In the San Juan Islands, Minkes have been seen passing, apparently without concern, a body length away from orcas, presumably residents. The two species have even been seen swimming together in Johnstone Strait.

In Japan, Minkes have been kept for short periods in aquaria, but whalers have had the main human impact in the west Pacific and elsewhere. Having depleted all populations of larger whales that they can legally hunt—and some that they can't—whaling nations have concentrated since the 1980s on killing off the estimated world population of half a million Minke whales.

The Rarer Whales

The northern right whale dolphin was the first new whale species to be discovered in the eastern Pacific. (Pitman)

When Michael Bigg managed the whale research program at Nanaimo's Pacific Biological Station, he was distracted one day by a stranded whale—just outside the building. It was one of the rare beaked whales, little known to scientists. He was able to photograph it, but it escaped and swam away before he could definitely identify it.

North America's Pacific coast is one boundary of a very large ocean; there are many other kinds of whales in it than the commonest species discussed in earlier chapters. In whaling days, when catcher ships brought back anything they could find that was legal and large, we gained a comprehensive knowledge of the distribution of the less common larger whales. Now that whaling has ended, our knowledge of larger whales is becoming outdated, but our knowledge of smaller species is improving as interest grows in marine mammals.

More people are looking for whales than ever before. As with birdwatchers, the more people look, the more rare species they find. Any time you are on the sea or walking by the shore, you have a small but definite chance of seeing a rarity. Like keen birdwatchers, persistent whale watchers study field guides to become capable observers, photograph their sightings to record key identification features and examine corpses cast up on the shore for the information they may yield.

By piecing together many fragments of information from scattered sources, we can compile a fascinating story of the rarer whales. You might be the one to fill a gap in the story.

Rarer dolphins

In addition to the Pacific white-sided dolphin, several other dolphins visit the east Pacific from time to time.

Risso's dolphin is named for the French naturalist Giovanni Antonio Risso, who sent a drawing and description of a specimen to the great naturalist Baron Georges Cuvier. The adult has a blunt head and a grayish or silverish body, usually with a multitude of scratches from the squid which form its principal prey. Risso's mainly occurs out to sea, but one was shot at Stuart Island near Prince Rupert in May 1964. More recent records include two strandings at Discovery Bay in eastern Juan de Fuca Strait in March 1975, and nearby at Port Angeles in October 1987.

The saddleback dolphin, with a yellowish or tan patch on its sides, earns its other name "common" off the coast of California.

False killer whales are uncommon on the west coast. (Pitman)

Farther north it is known only from one specimen washed ashore at Victoria, British Columbia in April 1953 and a second on the Washington coast. Also not uncommon in southern California waters, the bottlenose dolphin is patterned in gray. Many people are familiar with its appearance from seeing captive animals. The striped dolphin, a tropical species, has occasionally been recorded on the coasts of British Columbia, Washington, Oregon and southern California. Also tropical is the dark-backed rough-toothed dolphin, first known in the region from a skull found in Marin County, California and now known from other records.

The northern right whale dolphin generally occurs off California and is not uncommon in the north Pacific. Its name derives from its lack of a dorsal fin, a characteristic it shares with the unrelated right whale. Larger males grow up to 10 feet (3 m) long. The US Exploring Expedition of 1838 to 1842 took the type specimen 400 miles (643 km) off the mouth of the Columbia River and expedition naturalist Titian Peale described it. Titian was the son of famous naturalist and painter Charles Willson Peale, who became one of America's first photographers and a pioneer cinematographer. Sightings off British Columbia include Rod Palm's recent report of six dolphins 30 miles (48 km) off Tofino. Specimen records include one on the west coast of Vancouver Island and another two in Washington state. This dolphin is uncommon in inshore waters, though in 1977 there was an unconfirmed report of five in Puget Sound.

Pilot whales and false killers

The short-finned pilot whale and false killer whale are also members of the dolphin family.

Pilot whales reputedly led fishermen to fish. The short-finned is locally known as the pothead, a term which describes its blunt rounded head. At one point the northeastern Pacific form was regarded as a separate species and named after whaler Charles Scammon. Males are as long as 18 feet (5.5 m), with a gray patch behind the curved dorsal fin. Offshore reports of the species come

The short-finned pilot whale, or "pothead," is more commonly seen away from the land, but occasionally turns up close to shore. (Pitman)

from as far north as the Gulf of Alaska, and it occasionally wanders close to land, for example in Barkley Sound and the Strait of Juan de Fuca.

The false killer whale strongly resembles a smaller, all-black orca. Normally it lives in tropical and temperate oceans and is uncommon in West Coast waters, but it has been sighted as far north as the Aleutians and Prince William Sound. One was shot near Olympia, Washington in May 1937, and a group was seen in Puget Sound in May 1987. In 1987 a specimen was stranded in Carr Inlet in South Puget Sound, and around the same time another was stranded on Denman Island, the first recorded for Canada.

Belugas: wandering white whales

If someone claimed to have seen a beluga in Puget Sound, you might be inclined to question his drinking habits or wonder if a whale had escaped captivity. Yet there was a sighting in 1940—before captive whales were commonplace. Moreover, belugas are well known for turning up in surprising places. Scammon refers to a Russian report of one 700 miles (1125 km) up the Yukon River in 1863. Another swam 250 miles (400 km) up Europe's polluted Rhine in 1966.

The name beluga (sometimes spelled "belukha") derives from the Russian word for "white"; in English this elegant species is sometimes appropriately called the white whale. Its colour and its lack of a dorsal fin make this relative of the narwhal easy to recognize. It grows to about 16 feet (5 m). An arctic and subarctic species, its range is mostly north of the Aleutians. It occurs in

A beluga, or white whale, at the Vancouver Aquarium.

Cook Inlet on the south coast of Alaska, however, and groups appeared as far east as Yakutat Bay.

Belugas are usually on display in the Vancouver Aquarium; the first ones came from Alaska in 1967. In recent years the US Navy has studied their military potential in the Puget Sound area. As some whales have reputedly escaped, perhaps there will be other far-flung observations.

Beaked whales

Seven of the world's eighteen beaked whales have been reported in the eastern Pacific, including one first named little more than thirty years ago. The beaked whales are mid-sized toothed whales with long, cylindrical bodies, on which small triangular dorsal fins are placed well back. Their name comes from prominent beaks with few teeth in the lower jaw; some females have no teeth.

Largest and best-known in the region is Baird's beaked whale (*Berardius bairdii*), which was first recorded at Bering Island in the Aleutians. Its type specimen, in the US National Museum (part of the Smithsonian), is named for naturalist Spencer Fullerton Baird (1823–87), the museum's second secretary. Baird's is dark gray, sometimes with white patches underneath, and its lower jaw projects well beyond the upper. Baird's occurs offshore in schools of between ten and twenty in the summer months, ranging as far south as California. With a maximum length of 42 feet (13 m), Baird's was big enough to attract whalers when nothing else was available. Between 1948 and 1967, whalers brought twenty-four "bottlenose whales" into Coal Harbour on Vancouver Island. The stomachs of captured specimens, mainly males, contained rock-fish and squid. Strandings include one at Port Townsend, Washington in December 1962, and others in the Aleutians and British Columbia. Sightings include a report of three observed near Tofino in February 1996.

Stejneger's beaked whale (*Mesoplodon stejnegeri*) is another north Pacific species found between Alaska and California. The type specimen—a skull—was found by a Norwegian curator of the US National Museum, Leonard Stejneger, on Bering Island in 1883. Stejneger's is dark above and white below, with a brown saddle across the blowhole. A complete animal became available when a 17-foot (5 m) male was stranded in Yakima Bay, Oregon in 1904. Most reported strandings have been in the Aleutians, but there have been two British Columbia records. A skull was found near Port McNeill in 1953, and a stranded specimen at Tofino in 1959 was 12.5 feet (3.8 m) long. The Waatch River in Washington has also produced a specimen.

A skull found at Gray's Harbor in Washington in 1944 indicated the existence of a then unknown species of *Mesoplodon.* In the following year a better specimen was discovered at La Jolla, California. Its finder, Carl Hubbs (1894–1979), was a distinguished marine biologist of the Scripps Institute in California. He ascribed it to an existing species, but later study showed that it represented a new species which was named Hubbs' beaked whale (*Mesoplodon carlhubbsi*) in 1963. Hubbs' is black with a white top to the beak. We now know a few live in the north Pacific as far north as Prince Rupert. Even now, scientists know Hubbs' beaked whale from only about ten specimens, including a juvenile male washed ashore at Pacific Rim National Park in 1963.

Cuvier's beaked whale (*Ziphius cavirostris*) has been reported between the Aleutians and California. Cuvier's is varied in colour, and has a small head with a stubby beak. In British Columbia, skulls have been found at Bella Bella, Cape Scott and Victoria. Strandings occurred at Estevan Point, Jordan River, Langara Island and Sandspit, Queen Charlotte Islands.

Rarer species include Hector's beaked whale, known from four strandings in California and two sightings off the coast of that state. Blainville's beaked whale is known from one stranded female in San Mateo County, northern California, and the ginkgo-toothed beaked whale from a stranded female near San Diego.

Dwarf and pygmy sperm whales

Through the nineteenth century, these species were so little known that almost every new specimen was described as a new species under a different name. Only in the twentieth century did most scientists agree that there are only two species. Both belong to genus *Kogia*, whose name suggests how cetologists amuse themselves: the name reputedly translates the sound of the English slang term "codger," meaning a peculiar person, into Latin. Both species are deep gray above and paler beneath, and have a white curved mark at the sides of the head.

The pygmy sperm whale (*Kogia breviceps*) grows to about 11 feet (3 m), has up to sixteen pairs of teeth in the lower jaw but none in the upper, and has a strongly curved dorsal fin. Several strandings have occurred in Washington state: on the outer coast in May 1942, on Whidbey Island in October 1977 and at Port Angeles in June 1985.

The dwarf sperm whale (*Kogia simus*) grows to a maximum of 9 feet (2.7 m). It has fewer teeth in the lower jaw and sometimes two or three on each side of the upper jaw. In British Columbia there has been one stranding, at Bamfield in 1981. Others have been recorded in Puget Sound and on the coast of Oregon.

The spectacular sperm whale

"Without doubt, the largest inhabitant of the globe; the most formidable of all whales to encounter, the most majestic in aspect; and lastly, by far the most valuable in commerce." Thus Herman Melville described the sperm whale in his novel *Moby Dick*, the greatest work of literature inspired by the consuming human interest in whales.

Sperm whale teeth are pointed, to help the whale grip the squid that are its main prey. (DAES)

Melville was wrong about its size, but the spectacular sperm whale probably comes to mind when most people think of whales. It has been the chief prize of whalers for centuries, the subject of dramatic paintings of

Left: Herman Melville's favourite, the sperm whale, occurs offshore along the Pacific coast. (Pusser)
Below: A sperm whale heads for a deep dive, which may last as long as half an hour. (Baird)

conflict between whale and whaler or giant squid, the source of valuable, mysterious ambergris. No wonder this species has particularly captured our imagination. Yet the sperm whale is not a legend, but a real beast, and still occurs in our waters despite long years of whaling. Males have been recorded as long as 60 feet (18 m), though females usually grow only to 37 feet (11 m). The sperm's huge head, filled with spermaceti oil, dwarfs the narrow lower jaw, which alone bears impressive conical teeth. A single blowhole on the left side of its head blows forward and sideways; this alone is enough to identify a sperm whale at sea.

In summer, sperm whales occur offshore along the Pacific northwest coast from the Bering Sea southward. The females tend to stay farther south, and males leave the northern waters in winter. Of three whales marked off California in January, one was recovered off Washington in June, and another in the Gulf of Alaska in April. Between 1905 and 1966, whalers took more than 5,000 up to 200 miles (321 km) offshore in British Columbia waters, mostly around the Queen Charlottes. Most were mature males up to 46 feet (14 m). Each seemed to lead a school of up to thirty females and young. Occasionally sperm whales appear in inshore waters such as Dixon Entrance, Hecate Strait and Queen Charlotte Sound.

Studies of food show that Bering Sea sperm whales' stomachs may contain strange items: stones, rock, sand, a glass buoy, crabs, a coconut, deep sea sponge and cut flesh of a baleen whale. One sperm from California had a shoe in its stomach.

British Columbia specimens were reported to contain dogfish, ragfish, rockfish and skate, though the sperm's principal prey seems to be the squid *Moroteuthis robustus*, whose 4 foot (1.2 m) body may have tentacles over 11 feet (3 m) long.

The sperm dives deeply after its prey. Off British Columbia in 1932, an American cable-laying ship *All America* found a dead sperm tangled in a cable that had been at 3,330 feet (1,014m). Directional hydrophones have tracked much deeper dives elsewhere. On rare occasions, groups of sperm whales strand themselves, as at Florence, Oregon in June 1979.

Although many nations have stopped whaling, until recently Japan and Russia still hunted the sperm whale in the Pacific, taking a reported 7,000 each year. In its size and commercial importance the sperm resembles the few baleen whale species.

Sperm whales were the chief prize of whalers for centuries. (Folkens)

Rarer rorquals and right whales

Rare Mysticetes species also live in this region. Three of the world's remaining four rorquals (in addition to humpbacks and Minkes) have been recorded in Pacific Northwest waters, where the northern right whale also rarely occurs.

The blue whale, the largest living animal, once grew to 100 feet (30 m) and 160 tons (144 tonnes) in these waters. (Baird)

The elusive blue whale

The blue whale, largest of the rorquals, has phenomenal strength. A whaler out of Akutan, Alaska harpooned a blue that towed the steamer—with its engines running at half-speed reverse—at 4 miles an hour (6.4 kph) from 5 p.m. until 9 a.m. when it died.

The north Pacific blue, the region's biggest whale, never reach the size of Antarctic blues. The biggest documented off British Columbia was 86 feet (26.2 m). Dale Rice, a US marine mammal scientist based in Seattle, estimated the remains at 90 tons (82 tonnes) and the live weight at 101 tons (92 tonnes).

Blue whales, not often seen in the wild, until recently were best known from whaling-era research. In summer, blues usually swim in offshore waters between California and the Gulf of Alaska, occasionally beyond the Aleutians. They gather in the eastern Gulf of Alaska and south of the eastern Aleutians. Tagged whales are known to move throughout the area and across to the western Pacific. In winter, blues range southward from the west coast of Vancouver Island.

Blues travel singly or in small groups, but can be hard to distinguish from other large rorquals. Their blow is a thin column up to

The long back and small fin indicate a blue whale. (Baird)

40 feet (12 m) high, and they usually alternate several shallow dives at twenty-second intervals with a deep dive lasting as long as half an hour. The long back and small dorsal fin appear after the spout, and flukes barely show before the next dive. The colour is a dark blue-gray, mottled on the underside. North Pacific whalers sometimes called blues "sulphur-bottomed whales" from the yellowish cast caused on their underside by a growth of microscopic plants, diatoms.

The north Pacific blue's main food is a krill species (*Euphausia pacifica*) less than an inch (2.5 cm) long, though they eat other crustaceans. Blues feed mostly at or near the surface. Blue catches from British Columbia whaling stations used to peak in June and September, indicating a definite north–south migration. Blues have been fully protected in the region since the 1965 season. About 1,500 may remain in the north Pacific, indicating first recovery from the impact of industrial whaling. Even at their height of abundance, blues averaged only one whale per 20 square miles (52 km^2); today they are even more elusive.

The fall of the fin whale

The fin whale, during the twentieth-century whaling years, was the baleen whale most frequently taken off the British Columbia coast. By the 1960s it had almost disappeared, but since "commercial extinction" does not mean complete disappearance, the fin whale is still with us.

The fin's summer distribution (May to July) stretches from well north of the Aleutians, through the Gulf of Alaska—with concentrations in the Aleutians, around the Alaska Peninsula and in Prince William Sound—to off the Queen Charlotte Islands. Occasional specimens turn up farther south. Tagging has suggested that populations from both sides of the Pacific intermingle.

Fin whales usually travel offshore but have been seen in Hecate Strait, Queen Charlotte Sound and occasionally Queen Charlotte Strait. Through the 1960s, local people got to know one fin whale

resident off the north end of Vancouver Island until it was shot around 1970. Others visit the Puget Sound area. In 1930 one fin whale, trapped in a log boom, allowed visitors to walk on its back before it escaped. The only recent record from sheltered waters is of a dead fin whale pushed into Tacoma in 1985 by the bow of a freight vessel. Wintering populations occur off southern California; marking has identified these as whales that summer in the Pacific Northwest. Long-distance migrations are no problem for this species; one radio-tagged near Iceland made 181 miles (292 km) in one day. Although fins travel in groups of five to seven, a large individual can be hard to tell from a blue and a smaller one from the lesser baleen whales. Most observers note a tall thin blow, a small curved dorsal fin and perhaps the narrow tail ridge that led whalers to call the fin a "razorback." Flukes are rarely visible. If a fin whale shows its head, an asymmetrical dark gray and white pattern is characteristic.

An approaching fin whale shows its white jaw underwater, part of an asymmetric colour pattern which countershades it when it turns on its side to feed. (Baird)

The asymmetry of the colour pattern relates to the fin's feeding behaviour. It lunges at concentrated prey as other Mysticetes do, but the fin whale turns on its right side and swings on its right flipper while lunging. In this position, the dark left side and white lips on the right side maintain the whale's countershading, making it

Fin whales are not much smaller than blues. Their speed made them impossible for whalers to catch until steam catcher boats were invented. (Baird)

less obvious to its prey. In the Aleutians the fin eats sardines and pollack but elsewhere they browse on planktonic crustaceans.

The fin whale was the largest species eaten by the Makah and Quileute off the Olympic Peninsula, though aboriginal whalers may have taken this large species only when they found a dying whale floating. Steam-powered catchers equipped with modern whale gun and exploding harpoon could successfully hunt the fin, which became the staple of the hunt until its numbers fell. An estimated population of 45,000 Pacific fins by 1975 fell as low as 20,000, the estimated current population.

Oh sei can you sea

The sei whale (pronounced "say") is named after the pollack fish which appears on the Norwegian coast each year at the same time as the whale. The sei eats numerous species of fish, but will also eat squid and plankton such as copepods, common prey in northwestern waters. The sei skims through the surface water, sometimes turning on its side for a while like a fin whale, waving a flipper in the air. A large sei catches about one ton (900 kg) a day when actively feeding.

In summer, seis can be seen offshore from north of the Bering Straits to Baja California and from June to August frequently appear off Washington and Vancouver Island. In winter seis normally occur from California southward. A specimen marked off California in November 1962 was killed off Vancouver Island in August 1966.

The sei travels in small groups, apparently forming strong pair bonds. The quick-moving whale has a narrow blow only about 10 feet (3 m) high. With a maximum length in the Pacific of around

50 feet (15 m), an adult sei is bigger than a Minke but substantially smaller than a fin whale. It tends to surface horizontally and spends more time than a Minke at or just below the surface. The pectoral fins show no white, and the head pattern is symmetrical. White oval scars from lampreys or cookie cutter sharks are common.

Whalers largely ignored the sei, relatively low in blubber and oil, until larger species had been hunted near extinction. Then Vancouver Island whaling stations took it most frequently, reducing north Pacific populations to numbers that optimistic observers estimate at 20,000. No doubt for this reason, the sei's rare visits to inland waters have become even rarer since the 1960s. The average age of sexual maturity has also declined from ten years to six or seven.

The similar Bryde's whale has been reported off California.

Recovering right whales?

The right whale got its name from its value to early whalers. It was slow, relatively easy to kill and rich in oil; it floated when dead and had a mouth full of long baleen. In every sense it was the right whale to catch. Many of these features also endeared it to northern aboriginal peoples, for the right—and its arctic relative the bowhead—sustained humans in the most inhospitable climates.

Both species live in plankton-rich high Arctic waters, cruising slowly through surface waters catching crustaceans on their long narrow baleen plates. The bowhead is so adapted to the ice margins that it never comes south of the Aleutians (and so is not included in this book). The northern right whale has a more southerly range, summering in subpolar seas and wintering in temperate waters.

From a distance, a right is identifiable by its large V-shaped spout about 16 feet (4.9 m) high and its large body with neither dorsal fin nor ridge. At closer quarters, it may be possible to see the whitish bonnet and other barnacle-covered callosities on the black skin of the head, the arch of the lower jaw and sometimes on the back. The flukes lift in preparation for a dive. West Coast right whales are generally under 55 feet (17 m) long, though one Kodiak Island specimen reached 65 feet (20 m).

Archaeological sites around Puget Sound have yielded right whale remains. Historically, rights summered in the Bering Sea

and the Gulf of Alaska and as far south as Vancouver Island—a region whalers called the Kodiak Ground. Their winter range seems to have extended from waters off southern British Columbia and Washington state south to California. Breeding possibly took place in sheltered areas along the West Coast, though no one documented this when they could still study rights in their original range. Right whales were one of the earliest prey of north Pacific whalers, with predictable results. For a few years before 1851, as many as 400 ships were taking 1,500 to 2,000 right whales a year on the Kodiak Ground. By 1874 Scammon commented: "The whalemen of the Northwestern Coast made such havoc among these colossal animals...as to have nearly extirpated them, or driven them to some unknown feeding ground." The unknown feeding ground was a fantasy.

Right whales were not protected until the beginning of international co-operation in whale management in 1937, when scientists expected them to increase like the gray. There are records of twentieth-century right whales; a few still summer in the Gulf of Alaska in groups of as many as eight. Records from farther south are infrequent. In April 1959, two pods of eight each appeared 19 miles (30 km) off the coasts of Washington and Oregon, and in January 1967 a group of three swam near Cape Flattery, Washington. In 1983 two were sighted on the Swiftsure Bank at the Strait of Juan de Fuca entrance. Only a few even rarer stragglers have turned up south of Oregon. Current estimates place the

The finless back of the right whale is a rare sight after decades of illegal hunting in this century. (Baird)

world population at 1,000 to 4,000. Of the many that once lived here, only 100 to 200 survive in the northern Pacific.

Why have right whales been so slow to recover compared with other protected species? Rights probably mature at about ten years like other whales, though they may bear young only every three years. The food supply is still available, though perhaps competitively cropped by sei and fin whales. A clue lies in more than 100 sightings reported by Soviet and Japanese whaling boats between 1941 and 1968 in mid-Pacific, north of latitude 50—Vancouver Island—and west of longitude 150—the Alaska Peninsula. Cetologists have been suspicious of such reports. Since the fall of the Iron Curtain, Russian whale scientists have admitted that reported sightings of rare species were often actually killed whales. Instead of indicating a reviving species, the reports actually marked losses to the already slender right whale population.

West Coast Whaling

Humpback whale at the Coal Harbour whaling station circa 1960. (Hole)

The sleepy little hamlet of Coal Harbour, on Quatsino Sound near the northern end of Vancouver Island, has some commercial fishing but little to attract tourists. Yet the settlement has a remarkable past. Its whaling station—with other shore-based stations on Vancouver Island's west coast—took 22,695 whales in just fifty-six years. Coal Harbour, Canada's last shore station, was active from 1911 until 1967, the centennial year in which we celebrated our role as a modern nation.

Blue whale jaws remind Coal Harbour visitors of the community's whaling history. (DAES)

On the concrete ramp in front of the old flying station hangar, hundreds of whales were flensed, stripped of their baleen or teeth and boiled down into oil, leaving a reek that lingered on clothes and pervaded the air. Now, only hints of that history can be seen. The café is decorated with photographs of whale butchering, a silent harpoon gun is mounted in front of Moby Dick's Store, and nearby, the jaws of a blue whale make a backdrop for a memorable souvenir photo. When I visited Coal Harbour recently, I was able to connect within minutes with local people who had taken an active part in whaling or had grown up in the community.

Understanding whaling

Whaling, from earliest known times until the mid-twentieth century in the Pacific Northwest, was likely to be the principal human interest in whales. Aboriginal peoples on the outer coast have taken drifting whales and pursued living ones from dugout canoes for around a thousand years; the whale pervaded their culture. Sea-going European, American and Canadian travellers often came here seeking and then hunting commercially attractive whale stocks. No one knows for certain how many thousands of whales have been taken since the fishery began in the early 1800s, but partial records give an indication. Pelagic whalers, hunting from self-contained sailing ships based in France, England and New England, killed some 5,000 sperm whales each year in the Pacific.

Conservation of whales has been an active concern for only about three decades. It is easy for today's writers or readers to bring a contemporary consciousness to whaling history, metaphorically throwing up their hands at the wholesale destruction of what we now regard as beautiful and intelligent animals. Much harder is putting ourselves in the position of the whale hunters, so desperate for food or work that they would take on the most dangerous prey in the most difficult conditions. Seamen have always taken their lives in their hands, but whaling especially required the longest, most dangerous voyages in the worst weather.

This viewpoint shift is a worthwhile exercise; we can recognize that while some whalers—whaling skipper W. A. Hagelund calls them "the poor, the very hungry, and mostly, the very desperate of men"—were as brutal as any conquering army, they also showed courage, ingenuity and imagination. It was whalers who travelled into uncharted waters around the globe. They alone had extensive first-hand knowledge of whales; some whalers made greater contributions to whale science than "closet naturalists" who gave cumbersome Latin descriptions to species that they encountered only through accidental strandings of dead whales. Whalers also gathered information that enabled scientists to understand where whales lived and retroactively study their distribution and numbers.

Many whalers wrote books about their travels. Herman

A rare right whale at the Kyuquot whaling station in about 1910 was worth photographing. (BCARS 24881)

Melville was a Pacific whaler whose *Moby Dick* is recognized as one of the greatest works of literature; another was Charles Scammon, whose book *Marine Mammals*, first published in 1874, became the definitive guide to West Coast marine mammals for almost a century. But a lot of whalers were just ordinary people doing a tough job—to folks in Coal Harbour and places like it, whaling was just what you did.

To fully understand whaling, we need to realize that modern history would be different without it. Many criticize modern whaling as an ecologically unsound, wasteful means of producing dog food; it is not legitimate to dismiss historic whaling products as currently unfashionable items such as perfumes and corset stiffeners. Before kerosene was patented in 1854, many people depended on lamps fuelled by the oil of the sperm whale to light their evenings—perhaps much of the literature we value would not have been written without it. Before modern plastics and spring steel, flexible baleen was a material of remarkably diverse uses. Without whale oil lubricants, the industrial revolution would hardly have got off the ground.

Whaling words

Barrel—old measure used for whale oil, approximately 35 gallons (132 L).

Catcher—small ship equipped with a harpoon gun, used to catch whales and tow them to a factory ship or shore station.

Factory ship—large ship equipped as the mother ship of a fleet of catchers; could winch entire whale carcass up a stern slipway for processing.

Flense—to remove the blubber from a whale.

Flenser—a person whose job it is to remove blubber.

Harpoon—a spear thrown by hand or fired from a harpoon gun.

Harpoon gun—a gun mounted on the front of a catcher ship, designed to fire an exploding harpoon.

Pelagic—whaling on the open ocean without using a land base.

Scrimshaw—engraved whale teeth or bone; a traditional whaler's hobby.

Trying out—boiling the oil out of blubber and bones.

Try works—iron boilers on deck or shore for trying out.

A thousand years of whaling?

Strandings of living and dead whales probably inspired aboriginal whale hunting. A huge animal—floating helplessly or cast

Ready for the hunt. A Makah whaler about 1910, with his canoe, harpoon, and floats. (VMM)

ashore dead—provided abundant meat, oil, bone and other materials. Its lucky finder no doubt gained in status among his fellows. James Swan recorded such an occasion near Gray's Harbor, Washington in 1856. First Peoples had built a camp and "were all very busy at my arrival, securing the blubber, either to carry home to their lodges, or boiling it out on the spot."

West Coast First Nations went on to hunt whales by various methods. By contact times they had evolved a complex whaling culture, regarded as the most sophisticated in the world.

The beginning of aboriginal whale hunting is difficult to date. Bones discovered in archaeological digs indicate only that whales were consumed, not necessarily caught. Although harpoons suitable for whaling have also been found, it is not possible to tell if they were used for whales, seals or sea lions. Nevertheless, excavations have shown that people at Namu ate a small toothed whale between 6,000 and 5,500 years ago. At Yuquot, whalebone fragments and artifacts date to 1000 B.C., and toggle harpoons like those later used for whale hunting date to around 1000 A.D.

Historically, aboriginal whaling was widespread on the outer coast. In the far north the Inuit (Eskimo) of Alaska and the Canadian Arctic were (and still are) whale hunters. The Aleuts of the Aleutian Islands, like inhabitants of the western Pacific, used poison to take whales. Farther east, other Alaska aboriginal peoples were successful hunters; in 1831 a visiting naturalist calculated that they had killed 118 whales in the Gulf of Alaska and recovered 43. Tlingit and Kwakwa'ka'wakw (Kwakiutl) caught whales infrequently. The Nuu-chah-nulth (Nootka) of Vancouver Island's west coast pursued whales in 30-foot (9 m) dugout canoes, led by chiefs who alone were entitled to cast a harpoon. Canoes were painted with magical designs, such as the lightning snake Haitlik, then painted black so that the whale wouldn't see them. A millipede inserted in a hole in the prow was said to quiet the whale. The Makah and Quileute, speakers of the Nuu-chah-nulth language, are whale hunters who occupy the west coast of the Olympic Peninsula in Washington state. The Salish-speaking Quinault and Clallam, also whale hunters, live still farther south.

Whaler's village

In 1966 Richard Daugherty, an archaeologist, started excavations into the deep midden at Ozette, a Makah village site abandoned in 1930 on the west coast of Washington's Olympic Peninsula. A 230-foot (70 m) test trench cut through 13 feet (4 m) of occupation deposits was so full of huge whale bones that, once documented, they had to be sawn up and removed. As the dig progressed, Daugherty saw that a mud slide had covered a complete house, which was later dated to about 1580.

The house was a time capsule of a whale culture before contact with Europeans. It proved to be 70 feet by 45 feet (21 by 14 m), big enough to house between twenty and forty people. Between 1970 and 1973, more than 20,000 artifacts came to light. Several more houses were subsequently dug, ultimately yielding more than 55,000 artifacts.

Among many mundane objects were striking indicators of the whale culture. Bones from orca, gray, right, sperm, fin and blue whales were all present. Just outside the house lay a couple of whale skulls with a row of vertebrae. Whale ribs were penetrated by broken mussel shell harpoons, and inside a box, a whale harpoon lay carefully wrapped with its mussel shell blade in place. Most remarkable was a carved wood whale fin set with more than 700 sea otter teeth, some of them in a pattern representing a thunderbird perched on a whale. This may have been a ceremonial feast dish lid.

Makah hunters bring in a whale to be shared by the community, around 1910. (VMM)

In the bows a Makah hunter harpoons a whale in traditional style, while a second man holds a line already fast to the whale, about 1909. (VMM)

Poisoning whales

The Aleuts paddled their frail skin-covered *baidarkas* to hunt humpback, right and other whales with stone-tipped lances. Many reports state that they steeped their lance points in poison fermented from the roots of monkshood (*Aconitum columbianum*), a lethal relative of the buttercup. Its source was a closely guarded secret, masked by a story that it came from human corpses—scary enough to discourage the casual inquirer from asking too many questions. Although some anthropologists believe the poison had more ritual significance than effectiveness, some whales certainly died. If a whale drifted ashore, marks on the lance point identified its killer, who shared the carcass with the finder.

Nuu-chah-nulth whalers

The Nuu-chah-nulth liked to winter in "inside" villages where they had access to salmon runs, sheltered from the rigours of the outer coast. In spring they moved to "outside" villages in sheltered sites with access to the outer shores. Here they had access to a great variety of seafood, from tidepool creatures to gray and humpback whales and perhaps the occasional right whale.

A chief and six or eight men would head out to sea in a 35-foot (11 m) dugout canoe, accompanied by other canoes. The chief's harpoon would be an 18-foot (5 m) shaft of yew bearing a toggled head with a mussel shell blade. Lines were twisted from cedar bark fibre, and painted sealskin buoys were attached to slow the whale down. If the canoe successfully approached a whale, the chief would try to harpoon it just behind the left flipper.

Scammon described an unlocated First Nations whaling scene from his own observations: "As soon as the whale is harpooned it may dive deeply, but very little time elapses before the inflated seal skins are seen again. The instant they are seen...all dash with a shout and a grunt toward the object of pursuit. Now the chase attains the highest pitch of excitement, for each boat...crew must lodge their harpoon in the animal...in order to obtain a full share of the prize."

Once the whale was dead, a crewman would dive into the water, make holes in the whale's lips and sew its mouth shut to stop it from sinking. Then all the canoes would tow the whale

Twenty-five-year-old Archie Seymour, helped catch this sei whale at Alert Bay in 1905. (VMM)

laboriously back to shore. The village would welcome the successful chief with a feast, giving him a ritually prepared piece of the whale's back. Others would then be served in a way recognizing their contribution to the hunt or their rank in the community. Oil from the carcass would be used in cooking and traded to other nations.

Our chief struck a whale

In the early nineteenth century the Nuu-chah-nulth held captive an English sailor, John Jewitt. Excerpts from his published diary reflect the realities of First Nations whaling:

"...the chief went for a walk upon a high mountain, singing all the day for whales to come that he might kill them." (Nov 6, 1803)

"Our chief out whaling, struck one and was near to him one day and one night, and then his line parted. Returned and was very cross." (April 22, 1803)

"A canoe arrived...with 600 weight of blubber that was taken from a whale that had died at sea and was drived a shore by a gale of wind." (January 10, 1804)

"This day there were ten canoes out whaling, they stuck five whales, but their harpoons drawed, and they returned without having caught any." (April 8, 1804)

"Our chief's harpoon was made of a very large mussel shell, but so thin that as soon as he struck a whale the shell broke. I told him I could make a very good one out of steel, and should be as sharp as a knife; he ordered me to go to work upon it immediately, which I did." (April 10, 1804)

"About two o'clock, p.m. our chief struck a whale and killed him, about five o'clock he was towed by forty canoes into the cove. The chief was very much delighted with the harpoon I had made for him." (April 16, 1804)

"Employed at cutting up our chief's whale. The natives have now a great plenty, they eat twenty times in the course of a day. Our chief gave me an hundred weight of blubber, and told me I might cook it as I pleased, and I used to boil a piece of it with some young nettles which served for greens." (April 18, 1804)

A continuing tradition

As Americans and Europeans took up whaling and sealing, they found ready recruits among the First Peoples. Some aboriginal whalers stayed at home and continued to hunt in the traditional way, however. The Nuu-chah-nulth hunted a whale near Tofino in

1909, and the Makahs were photographed hunting from a dugout canoe in 1910; both groups have taken the occasional whale since then. Whales have continued to provide important subsistence in the far north, where Inuit whaling is practised to the present day. In the late 1990s, the Makah had permission from the International Whaling Commission to take up to five whales, and were again actively hunting.

Thar she blows!

Aboriginal whaling shows us how modern commercial whaling started, and similar customs survive in Europe; Faroe Islands whalers drive small toothed whales into shallow water where they can kill them. The Norse began catching big whales as early as 890 and took their skills to Normandy. The Basques were using these skills by the tenth century to catch right whales in the Bay of Biscay, trying them out at shore stations. They in turn spread their expertise through the maritime nations of Europe, furthering the development of north Atlantic whaling. Indeed, Basque whalers were active shortly after Cartier explored the St. Lawrence; as early as 1540 they had a thriving whaling settlement at Red Bay, now in Labrador. As whales accessible from shore became rarer, whalers brought back only baleen or learned to cut up whales at sea, making it possible to hunt farther afield. For centuries, the whales were tried out on the nearest land or back at the home port. The risk of fire on wooden ships was so great that no one risked trying out on a ship until about 1750, when brick furnaces reduced the danger to a more acceptable level.

A gunner ready to shoot. (VMM)

As the world centre of whaling shifted to New England, the great days of pelagic whaling began. The sperm became a primary prey, but no whale was safe unless—like the great rorquals—it was too fast to catch. A spotter sat in a masthead crow's nest on each sailing ship. The cry of "Thar she blows!" spurred frantic launching of small boats which pursued the whale until the harpooner could make fast a line to the boat.

The whale's response—readily described in picturesque terms—determined the hunt's success. If he "sounded," the line might have to be cut before the boat was pulled under; his "flurry" might lead to a "stove boat"; the crew might be towed rapidly along the surface in a "Nantucket sleighride" until they feared losing their boat or their lives. As the whale tired, the crewmen would again pull forward and try to fix further harpoons or kill it with lance thrusts, until its "chimney was on fire"—its spout mingled with blood. If the whale was killed, it was laboriously towed to the ship. Even the buoyant right whales occasionally sank, like the one that "to pay us for 4 hours hard pulling...went down like so much lead, taking with him 4 harpoons and a lance." At the ship, flensers peeled a spiral "blanket piece" of blubber off the entire carcass, cut the rest to pieces from a platform over the side and tried it out in the furnaces. Ships did not usually return to port, sometimes for several years, until their holds were filled with casks of whale oil.

Pelagic whaling in the northwest

As the sperm fishery got under way, Captain Cook and other early explorers on the northwest coast were noting whales and their use by First Nations. Their reports intrigued businessmen and politicians back home. English traders soon arrived in the area, precipitating conflict with the Spanish who had already laid claim to the west coast of the Americas. The 1790 Nootka convention resolved this by formally opening West Coast waters more than 30 miles (48 km) offshore to English whalers. This in turn precipitated Pitt the Younger into a political crisis, when he was accused of using the rather doubtful Spanish threat to Pacific whaling as an excuse to spend millions on the navy. A cartoon was published showing him "fishing for whales off Nootka Sound," and the government offered a bounty to whale ships to encourage them to fish the Pacific.

The Pacific was soon a major destination of whalers—Yankee, British, French, Dutch, German and some from the Canadian maritime provinces. They fanned out across its wide waters, taking whales as far as Japan. They soon discovered the advantages of Hawaii and many other islands as sources of supplies and labour and as places to recuperate from the strains of the hunt and cautiously exchange information.

Cutting up a sperm at Kyuquot whaling station, on the west coast of Vancouver Island in about 1910. (BCARS 24880)

It is not clear who was the northwest coast's first commercial whaler; there are English, French and Yankee contenders for the honour. Strong claimants include a British whaler (which did not catch any whales) in 1834; Captain Narcisse Chaudière of the *Gange* of Havre, who killed seven right whales—the largest quoted as 97 feet (30 m) long—in 1835; and Captain Folger of the *Ganges* (by coincidence) of Nantucket the same year.

Many more followed. Yankee whalers increasingly dominated; by 1842 they operated 652 whaling ships of a world total of 882. Their crews were from New England, mixed with Black Americans, Portuguese from the Cape Verde Islands and Hawaiians (then known as Kanakas) from the Sandwich Islands. Though some were earnest religious men or temperance advocates, many more were foolish adventurers, drunks, petty criminals or worse. Not all whalers survived their trips, and obituaries—"dead from illness, dead after falling from aloft, dead by drowning, dead by whale"—give a pithy indication of the hazards of the trade.

For those who survived everyday hazards, the joys of bad weather and pumping leaky ships helped to fill time. Rewards were small—a tiny share of the voyage's profits. In the face of harsh treatment many a whaleman—like Melville—was tempted to jump ship, while others mutinied.

Early whaling was inefficient. One mid-nineteenth-century writer recorded: "The havoc they make of whales is intense. I have heard of one ship that sunk twenty-six whales after she had killed them; of another that killed nine before she saved one; of another that killed six in one day, and all of them sunk." As early as 1846 there were signs of overfishing, when a fleet of 263 vessels came back with an average of only 953 barrels of oil each.

As long as whalers could find a new supply of whales, they didn't see the decline as a problem. By 1843 they had started to take bowheads in the Bering Sea and from 1848 until around 1900 pursued them past the Bering Straits. Alternating bowhead and sperm in different seasons, they initially used Hawaii as a base. In 1855 Scammon discovered the breeding lagoons of the gray whale and thus another profitable—if short-lived—source of revenue.

New technology

Whaling was not new to the Hudson's Bay Company, which had equipped a whaling ship in eastern Canada as early as 1719. In 1842 Sir George Simpson, former head of the HBC, kept a keen eye on whaling prospects during his Pacific travels. He envisaged Camosun (later Victoria), the company's new west coast trading

The blubber has been stripped off this whale, and the meat is being cut up. (Sarjeant)

base established in 1843, as a base also for further HBC whaling.

The older city of San Francisco was supplying a few whale ships but rapidly became unpopular with captains during the 1849 gold rush, as whole crews would desert to try their luck. As gold fever died down, San Francisco became home port for captains including Scammon. When the transcontinental railway reached the city in 1869, it became even more attractive; it was now less necessary to sail the dangerous passage round Cape Horn. Pacific whaling found its home base on the west coast, first in San Francisco, later in Seattle and Victoria. Commercial shore whaling for grays began in California in 1846, creating a model that others eventually copied all along the coast.

During this period, the technology of destruction was improving with the development of a toggle harpoon, developed in 1848 by New England Black blacksmith Lewis Temple from an Inuit model. In 1858 a bomb lance was developed, which could be fired from a shoulder gun.

By 1864 Svend Foyn's modern harpoon gun was in use in Norway. A few years later whalers mounted it on a steam-powered boat large enough to carry it successfully and catch the rorquals, the fastest whales, which had hitherto been spared the efforts of whalers. Foyn's gun did not reach the New World for some time, however.

The West Coast's first successful steam whaler was operating from San Francisco in 1880. The *Mary & Helen*'s combination of sails and steam, by ensuring safer navigation in difficult waters near the arctic ice, stimulated a revival of interest in whaling in the north.

San Francisco continued as a base for Arctic steam whaling and Seattle soon joined it, sending out such ships as the remarkable *Mary D. Hume*, launched in Oregon in 1881. The ship worked out of Herschel Island in the high Arctic for many years and still served as a tug in Puget Sound in the 1970s.

Modern shore whaling depended upon small catcher ships powered first by sail and steam, later by steam or diesel, which ranged as far as possible in search of whales. A crowsnest on the forward mast allowed them to spot whales, and a harpoon gun mounted on the bow allowed the gunner (usually a Norwegian) to shoot an exploding harpoon into the whale, killing it quickly. Once it had killed two or three whales, the catcher brought in the whales to a processing station built in a sheltered spot accessible from the ocean, preferably upwind and distant from any community which would complain about the stench. The whales were winched up a slip and quickly butchered. The station rendered blubber, meat, and bones, and processed the oil by various new techniques into an enormous diversity of products.

Hunting humpbacks in Saanich Inlet

Saanich Inlet today borders some of the most populous areas of southern Vancouver Island. Few residents, gazing out at its quiet waters, can be aware that a century or so ago, weather permitting, they could have watched whalers catch humpbacks in the same spot.

The Hudson's Bay Company did not develop a west coast whaling fleet, but Victoria—the city which developed around Fort Camosun—became an important whaling base. In 1866 a Scot named James Dawson struck three humpback whales in nearby Saanich Inlet but failed to bring them in. Two years later, trying again with new partners in the schooner *Kate*, he killed eight whales despite thick fog. Meanwhile, Thomas Roys, an ingenious whaleman who invented a whaling rocket and a "whale raiser" to lift whales that had sunk in shallow water, came to Victoria in 1867. A year later he rented the steamer *Emma* but failed to bring in any whales.

For the next few years, the two rivals and their fluctuating groups of partners and competitors vied for the whales of the British Columbia coast. Roys promoted a company and built a whaling station on Barkley Sound, but had little success and left the area. He returned to Barkley Sound in 1870 for a second attempt and in 1871 brought a new ship, the *Byzantium*, from the Sandwich Islands (Hawaii). He attempted to establish a station in the Queen Charlottes, losing his ship in the process. In the meantime, Dawson and his partners moved operations to Cortes Island in the Strait of Georgia, suffered a shipwreck and lost whales to First Nations people, but managed some success. By the end of 1870, three companies had taken thirty-two whales, yielding 25,800 gallons (97,653 L) of oil, but low prices soon discouraged the would-be whalers.

Whaling activity remained low in British Columbia even when Samuel Foyn, nephew of the celebrated inventor, brought his uncle's patents and expertise to the West Coast in 1898. Although he promised he could set out from Vancouver and return in six hours towing a whale, he did not secure any financial backing,

Whaling ships of the "rainbow fleet" up for sale in 1947. Most of the ships went for scrap. (VMM)

since all the speculative money was tied up in the still profitable fur seal fishery.

Shore whaling succeeds

In 1904 the government of Canada passed new legislation requiring licensing of whaling stations. The new law also demanded that stations be 50 and later 100 miles (80 to 160 km) apart. British Columbia's first applicant was sealer Sprott Balcom, founder of the Pacific Whaling Company, for a station at Sechart—near Sechart Channel, Barkley Sound—on Vancouver Island's wild west coast. Once the station was built, Bascom brought in British Columbia's first catcher, the *Orion*, around the Horn from Norway. Over the next few years, Bascom and others established a string of other stations. In 1908 the catchers took 592 whales, 462 of them humpbacks.

In 1908 New York researcher Roy Chapman Andrews visited two Canadian whaling stations and later wrote a book describing their work. "The flesh was torn from the bones in two or three great masses by the aid of the winch, and the skeleton disarticulated.

After the bones had been split and the flesh cut into chunks two or three feet square, they were boiled separately in great open vats...When the oil had been extracted, the bones were crushed...making bone meal to be used as a fertilizer, and the flesh...was converted into a very fine guano...the blood was boiled and dried for fertilizer. Finally the water in which the blubber had been tried out was converted into glue."

For a while the business thrived. Five more catchers—the "rainbow" fleet of *Green, Black, White, Brown* and *Blue*—arrived in Victoria from Norway in 1911, and Balcom's company—now Canadian North Pacific Fisheries—built an ambitious station at Rose Harbour in the Queen Charlottes. With other partners he built another station at Gray's Harbor, Washington.

Akutan and Smellstrong

Norwegians, with the help of Foyn's patents, increasingly dominated the whaling industry worldwide. They soon saw an opportunity in Alaska, which was less regulated than British Columbia. Different groups established the United States Whaling Company, which built a station in Port Armstrong—soon nicknamed "Smellstrong"—on Baranof Island near Sitka in 1911, and the Alaska Whaling Company, which built a station at Akutan in the Aleutians in 1912. The Tyee Whaling Company of San Francisco opened another station on Admiralty Island in 1907. Bay City station in Washington state processed 2,698 whales, mainly fin and

The Akutan whaling station in the Aleutian Islands was established in 1912. Note the barrels of whale oil along the wharf. (BCARS 72493)

humpback, between 1911 and 1925.

Once again success was short-lived, as the available whale populations quickly dwindled. Admiralty Island closed in 1913 and Sechart in 1917, soon followed by Rose Harbour. A little whaling lingered until World War II, however, when Akutan eventually became an American military base after Pearl Harbor.

Ambergris

Coal Harbour's most dramatic find was a sperm whale containing 700 pounds (317 kg) of ambergris, which was marketed over a period of five years at seven to twelve dollars an ounce. Ambergris forms in the intestines of a few sperm whales—no more than 2 percent of those caught commercially—when it accumulates around the undigested beaks of cuttlefish. Mainly composed of nonvolatile alcohols, it was once enormously valuable in perfume manufacturing. A lucky find was often enough to convert a disastrous voyage into a profitable one. Ambergris still has a medical use in controlling spasms. The largest piece on record came from an Antarctic sperm and weighed 925 pounds (420 kg).

The last shore station in British Columbia was Coal Harbour. Established in a wartime Royal Canadian Air Force marine station in 1948, it was run by a number of different companies and partly owned in Japan after 1962. As many as six catcher ships served it before it finally closed in September 1967. At most the station employed eighty-five people in the plant—mostly transient workers who lived in a bunkhouse—and another seventy on the ships. Coal Harbour's products included meat, of which the best quality went to Japan, while poorer quality meat became pet food and stock feed. The plant also produced a fine machine oil; at one point a US tanker came to get a load for the US military.

Harry Hole, whaler

"You never forget the smell," grinned Harry Hole as he waved a small uncorked bottle of whale oil under my nose. "Sometimes the dog unearths an old whale bone and comes home with the smell clinging to him. Takes me right back."

This large rorqual has been pulled up the slip at Coal Harbour, ready for cutting up, around 1960. (Hole)

There was pride in his words. Though whaling now is considered horrific, thirty years ago there was pride in a job well done, pride in a working town with jobs for everyone, pride in work achieved efficiently and quickly before the meat spoiled and pride in raising strong healthy families in an isolated community with no outside help.

Harry Hole currently manages a water taxi and boat charter business, but as a younger man he worked on the whale boats.

"It was just like peeling a banana," he said. On cue his wife Pat brought out the photo album she had put together of Coal Harbour's history. Harry pointed to a photo of the flensing operation where men were stripping blubber from a sperm whale. "We could do a whale an hour." He looked piercingly at me, willing me to understand a different perspective and pride in an earlier way of life.

"You didn't question either ethics or conservation—it was just what you did. This plant took 50 percent of the whales taken on the west coast of North America, 300 in the first year, then up to 600 to 1,000 whales a season. These were the days when you could go out and see 100 whales at one time. We hunted as far down as the US border and up as far as the Charlottes."

Records show a successful and well-managed operation that processed blue, sperm, fin, sei, humpback, bottlenose and—with permits—gray whales. They even had a contract to take one killer whale for the Disney Corporation, which wanted a complete carcass—for reasons unknown to the catchers. Then Harry's voice became bitter. "In the last years things changed. Suddenly three Japanese and three Russian factory ships were offshore in competition. They admitted to taking 24,000 whales in one season. That's what finished us. We weren't the ones overfishing. Besides, it wasn't all bad. A lot of heart research was done on whales. We had ten top doctors here for two months and they said they learned more at the whaling station than in two years elsewhere." —AJS

Although Canada and the US are no longer whaling nations (apart from limited aboriginal hunts), whales that live in our seas were being taken after 1967. With the aid of factory ships, a fleet of catchers can function anywhere in the world. Despite attempts to limit commercial whaling, a few nations still use such ships and—until at least twenty years after Coal Harbour closed—were still actively whaling in the Pacific.

A Russian catcher ship mounts a gun on its bows capable of firing a 250-pound (112-kg) exploding harpoon. (Weyler)

7

Studying Whales

A breaching humpback is one of nature's most spectacular sights. (Folkens)

In 1908 Roy Chapman Andrews, a scientist at the American Museum in New York, arrived to study whales at the Sechart whaling station. The multinational workers greeted him with suspicion. On his first day a humpback was on the slip and "one of the cutters called me over to the side of the whale. As I bent down to examine the spot he pointed out, he thrust a huge knife into the belly. Out shot a stream of blood, almost black, and a horrible odor. Both struck me fair in the face. I went over on my back, slid down to the slip and into the water. All the six nationalities screamed with delight in its own particular national way; the station whistles blew and the bells rang:...they figured the "professor" had passed for I never had more accommodating men to work with from that time on."

Thus the whalers impressed their superior knowledge on the "professor" in a scene symbolic of many encounters between workers with practical knowledge and scientists with theoretical knowledge. Whales—more than most creatures—have always attracted two kinds of experts. On one side First Nations whale hunters, sailors, explorers, whalers and (more recently) whale watching skippers have gathered the practical knowledge of whale biology and behaviour they need to find, catch or interpret whales. Their expertise is recognized by cetologist Roger Payne in "My own law: any observant local knows more than any visiting scientist. Always. No exceptions."

On the other side are those whose knowledge is largely theoretical—"closet naturalists," measurers of bones, compilers of information, and writers of taxonomic papers, scientific texts and management studies—people who often have a better grasp of scientific method and better access to information from long ago and far away, but whose opportunities to test their information against real experience may be limited by the demands of profession or family.

The best work has often been done by those lucky, persevering, dedicated individuals who have been able to combine both types of knowledge in a meaningful way—the rare whalers like Scammon who took the trouble to study and write about their experience, or museum scientists like Andrews who got abundant field experience. More recently, a few scientists have emerged who are either adequately funded or feel long hours of field work with the whales are more important than tenure and a regular paycheque; much of the most exciting whale research is in their hands.

To extend the bounds of science

When the first scientific expeditions reached the northwest coast, they had some knowledge of whales, which were known to sailors and scientists on both sides of the Atlantic. Their reports spoke of great numbers of whales—enough to excite commercial interests—but said little of which species were present, or of their anatomy, physiology and behaviour. A primary objective of the US Exploring Expedition of 1838 to 1842 was to support "important interests of our commerce embarked in the whale-fisheries, and other adventures in the great Southern Ocean." Consequently, its itinerary was to visit major whaling grounds in the Pacific Ocean and the Antarctic Seas, and its staff was instructed to "take all occasions...to extend the bounds of science, and promote the acquisition of knowledge."

The expedition visited the northwest coast and travelled widely in the Pacific, collecting hundreds of birds and other vertebrates, but did little scientific work on whales. Its main contribution was to take back a few small species of porpoises which expedition naturalist Titian Peale described. The only cetacean from our area was the northern right whale dolphin.

Although it collected few whales, the US Exploring Expedition took back many specimens for which no long-term provision had been made. The need to house and study this material was an important stimulus to establishing the Smithsonian Institution, America's national museum complex, which has done much to document and preserve physical evidence of whales.

Minke in the museum

The world's largest animals often present an insuperable challenge to natural history museums, whose basic role is to collect and preserve physical evidence of living things. Each species' type specimen is the fundamental specimen—the first named or designated specimen which becomes a permanent point of reference for a species. Yet for many whale species, we lack designated type specimens. The huge size and weight of the bones of large whales prohibits most museums from collecting, storing and exhibiting more than a token bone or two. As a result, most people have little real idea of the size of a large whale.

The senior museum in the Pacific Northwest, now the Royal

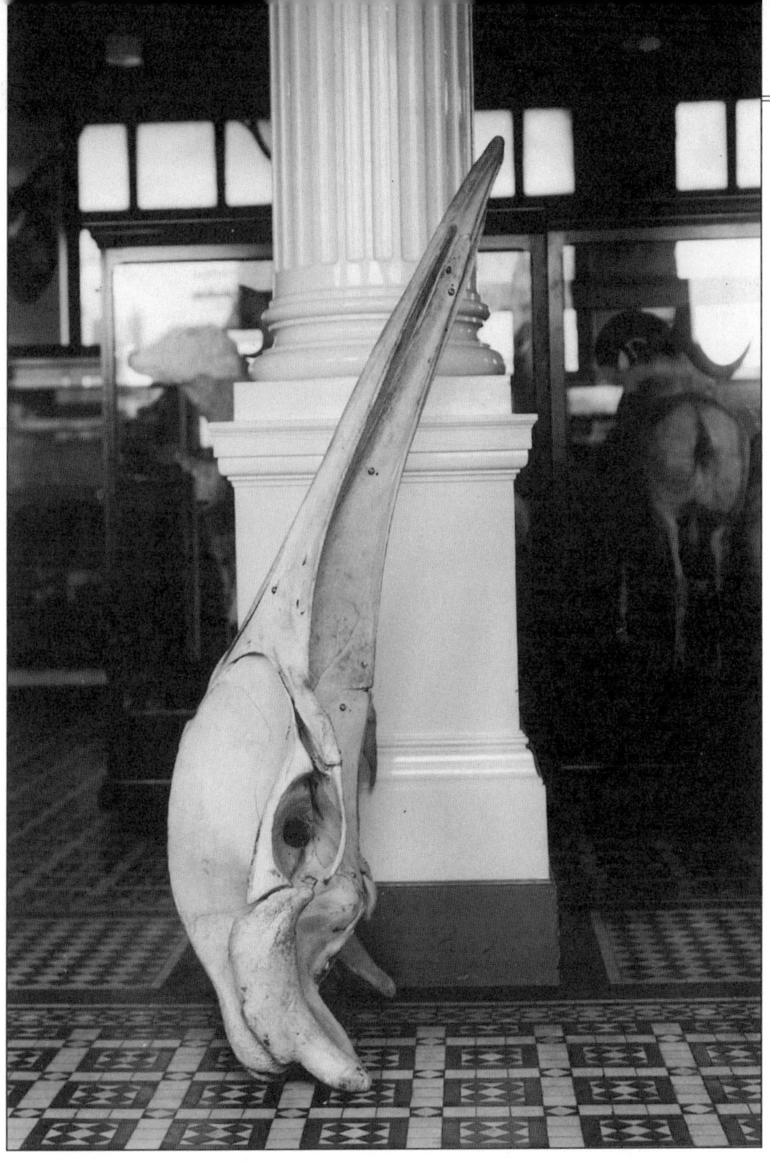

This Minke skull was the first collected for the BC Provincial Museum in 1937. (McTaggart-Cowan)

British Columbia Museum in Victoria, opened in 1886 but acquired a whale skeleton only in 1937. A Minke drowned in a salmon trap at Sooke, west of Victoria; the specimen was sent to the museum on a barge. Museum assistant Ian McTaggart Cowan and his wife Joyce received the whale on a warm Saturday and felt that "immediate action was required." Together they measured and dissected the carcass and moved the skeleton to the museum laboratory for cleaning and degreasing.

The few museums able to pursue whale research did so with the help of commercial whaling. When shore whaling began in British Columbia, it attracted the interest of Roy Chapman Andrews.

Roy Chapman Andrews

Andrews (1884–1960) is the real prototype of the fictional Indiana Jones. Fresh out of college in 1906, he talked himself into a job sweeping the floors at the American Museum of Natural History. He helped construct a life-size model whale and soon afterward collected a dead 54-foot (16 m) right whale on Long Island. When he tried to describe his find later, Andrews found little useful information in the scientific literature and decided "here was the most extraordinary group...in the entire animal kingdom just waiting for someone to expose its secrets." The museum had just received a donation to support whale research, and Vancouver Island's whaling stations had recently opened.

By 1908 Andrews was on the Pacific coast, having volunteered to work without salary if the museum would pay his expenses. He persuaded the whaling company to help him and had a rough passage to Sechart—"Great Scott, wasn't I sea-sick." After his unplanned bath, Andrews tried frantically to measure the whale "but I had to step lively to get what I wanted before the carcass disappeared," as the flensers attacked it even before it left the water.

Andrews measured and dissected whales, and went out on the catchers to study living whales as they were pursued and shot. He went on to Alaska and later the Dutch East Indies, Korea and Japan; for a while he became the reigning expert on whales of the north Pacific. He participated in the posthumous birth of a 22-foot (7 m) finback, observed mating humpbacks and escaped being crushed by half a whale only by leaping off a dock into 20 feet (6 m) of water.

Horrified by the scale of destruction of the whales, he saw no other easy way to study these far-travelling mammals. "It is deeply to be regretted," he said, "that the wholesale slaughter of whales will inevitably result in their early commercial extinction, but meanwhile science is profiting by the golden opportunities given for the study of these strange and interesting animals."

All his travelling, collecting and recording was productive scientifically, for Andrews gathered data and sent whale skeletons back to New York from all around the north Pacific. He rediscovered the western Pacific gray whale and published monographs on that and other species. He wrote *Whale Hunting with Gun and Camera*, a popular book on Pacific whales which first appeared in 1916. While doing this research, he fell in love with the East. His major expeditions into Mongolia—with particular success in discovering dinosaurs—brought fame which eclipsed his decade of whale work. He finished his professional life as director of his museum and spent his retirement writing books about nature and his travels.

Immatures and insulin

Whaling stations in Alaska and British Columbia also had visits from government scientists such as Victor Scheffer of the US Biological Survey, and Ian McAskie and Gordon Chesley Pike of Canada's Fisheries Research Board. The steady stream of dead whales at least gave them some information about whale anatomy, biology and population structure.

Victor Scheffer joined the Survey in 1937 and almost immediately joined the Aleutian Islands Expedition. In the next two years he visited the Akutan station, one of few still functioning. Researchers were studying the size of whales caught (management required protecting the younger whales) and collecting stomach contents to find out what the whales ate. From the University of Washington campus in Seattle, Scheffer continued his research and taught at the university, travelling the West Coast whenever he had the chance. He published several books on marine mammals and served as chairman of the Marine Mammal Commission.

Keepers at lighthouses, such as the Georgina Point light on Mayne Island, reported marine mammal sightings to the Fisheries Research Board in the 1960s. (DAES)

Canada signed the International Whaling Convention in 1946, involving the federal government in the management of whale stocks in Canadian waters and requiring the reporting of statistics to the international body. The Fisheries Research Board's Pacific Biological Station in Nanaimo, established in 1908, eventually became the base of limited research on Pacific whales that continues to this day, though since 1960 most Canadian whale research has been based at the Arctic Biological Station in Quebec. Gordon Pike documented whales brought in to Coal Harbour throughout the life of the station, recording data about size, sex, species and stomach contents required by the International Whaling Commission. He also acquired material for biological study and studied parasites in an attempt to trace whales' movements into warmer waters. An important investigation examined reproductive organs to ascertain the maturity of the whales caught; this revealed that 50 percent of fin whales and 35 percent of humpbacks were immature.

Many regular collaborators—including lighthouse keepers, the navy, and crews of lightships, oceanographic research vessels and weather ships—compiled data on marine mammals in special logbooks supplied by the Fisheries Research Board. Many casual reporters brought stranded whales and other observations to the attention of the FRB scientists. In 1969 Pike—with Ian McAskie—completed a study of this and other data, published as *Marine Mammals of British Columbia*. This is still the most comprehensive account of the whales of British Columbia waters. After Coal Harbour was closed down, Pike was transferred to the Montreal office and within two years took his own life. His ashes were scattered in Nanaimo's Departure Bay.

Thousands of people enjoy seeing orcas in Vancouver Aquarium, but few are aware of the scientific research conducted behind the scenes.

The Fisheries Research Board also pioneered co-operative research on whales. For instance, it published specialized studies by Ira Cornwall, a Victoria amateur oceanographer who became a self-taught expert studying barnacles, including those that parasitize whales. More commercially, the board's Vancouver experimental station studied the feasibility of extracting insulin, vitamins and other pharmaceutical products from whales.

An unexpected orca

The growth of aquaria gave researchers better access to smaller living whales. Soon after its opening, the Vancouver Aquarium began research on fish, but it seemed impracticable to do much on whales, and the first captive orca in 1964 was an accident. The aquarium planned to obtain a dead orca specimen as a model for a sculpture and to permit brain research by Dr. Patrick McGeer, professor of neurochemistry at the University of British Columbia's School of Medicine.

Somewhat unexpectedly, the aquarium ended up with the first live orca—soon named Moby Doll—to be displayed anywhere. It became the focus of quite different research: biomedical investigation of conditions necessary to keep an orca alive and healthy in captivity. An impressive university and hospital team was able to keep Moby Doll alive for nearly three months and learned enough for the aquarium to show orcas almost continuously ever since. Moby's recorded underwater vocalizations confirmed that orcas used echolocation.

By the following year a new orca, Skana, was in residence, and the aquarium could start research that only regular access to a living whale made possible. By 1968, with funding from the aquarium and the University of British Columbia, animal psychologist Paul Spong had been hired to research "problem solving behaviour and intelligence in the porpoise and killer whale."

Skana on strike

How does one study a laboratory animal weighing several tons when it refuses to co-operate? In 1968 animal psychologist Paul Spong faced this interesting problem.

He was doing experiments on visual discrimination on Skana, the Vancouver Aquarium's orca. Pairs of cards marked with either one or two lines were lowered into the water, and when Skana pushed the lever selecting the double line she was rewarded with half a herring. After hundreds of experiments, Spong discovered that Skana was 90 percent successful on discriminating double lines down to a sixteenth of an inch (2 mm) apart. In the best scientific tradition, Spong repeated the experiment to improve the statistical validity of his results—only to find that Skana chose the wrong answer—eighty-three times!

After much thought, Spong decided that perhaps Skana was "on strike"—bored with visual stimulus when noise was of more interest—and turned to experiments with music and other sounds. Later, sitting on the edge of the pool, Skana scared him by running her teeth gently over his bare feet. After hastily withdrawing his feet, Spong courageously returned them. Skana repeated the behaviour eleven times, until Paul was able to resist the impulse to pull out his feet at her approach. Laboratory animals were not supposed to behave like this. It was some time before it dawned on Paul that Skana was training him. He wrote later, "She had very effectively and quickly deconditioned my fear of her."

Paul's experiments led him not just to interesting scientific results, but to a whole new view of the intelligence of whales—and thus to question the appropriateness of keeping orcas in captivity. After a breach with the aquarium, he became a driving force in Greenpeace's campaign to save the whales.

Aquarium research

What is the aquarium's role in research? "The aquarium has not always put energy into research or facilitating research," explained John Ford, who is research scientist (marine mammals) and also cross appointed at the University of British Columbia (see photo page 31). "It has whales because people want to see whales, but it costs to keep them. The aquarium is the only self-supporting cultural institution of its size in the country, but it barely breaks even every year. Our research is funded by the whale adoption program.

An aquarium is the easiest way to study whales such as this orca underwater. (DAES)

"There is still research that can only be done in aquaria," John continued. "Some is management oriented—we have developed milk formulas for calves, and studied the endocrinology of reproduction, and we did the first paternity test for orcas."

Another example of research possible only in aquaria is the series of monthly blood samples that Dave Huff, the aquarium's vet, took during Bjossa's long captivity. This has built a database of normal blood chemistry for a killer whale.

But research is not just management oriented. Despite the difficulties, the aquarium has supported a number of cetacean research projects. Best known is John's own important work on orca acoustics (discussed in Chapter 2). Other completed or ongoing projects involve dolphins, belugas' hearing ability and narwhal acoustics. John cites advantages of aquaria. "You can't do much with physiology in the wild, and 99 percent of the whale sonar work has been done in a captive setting. However, we try to merge wild and aquarium studies."

John Ford has now developed a project called Whale Link with the assistance of BC Tel and computer science students at the BC Institute of Technology. Orcas swimming past permanent hydrophones activate cellular phones which automatically call the aquarium and broadcast the whales' calls. There the orcas can be identified and tracked. You can tune in to Orca FM at the aquarium or in the Johnstone Strait area.

A short-finned pilot whale. (Baird)

Whales in the wild

In 1946 British Columbia Provincial Museum director Clifford Carl received reports of an albino female killer whale off Race Rocks and named her Alice. Recognizing an opportunity to keep track of an individual whale, he sought assistance from lighthouse keepers, fishermen, fisheries patrol staff and the Royal Canadian Mounted Police. By 1959 Carl had more than seventy records from points all around Vancouver Island and recognized that people were observing more than one albino. He obtained photographs of one individual.

This pioneer effort emphasized the importance—and the difficulty—of following individual whales' movements. "The cost of keeping watch on an animal that ranges freely across an ocean is prohibitive," said Ian McAskie of the Fisheries Research Board. At one point he worked from Coal Harbour "on one of the killer boats to see if I could mark some young sperm whales with a specially designed dart." He fired it from a shotgun into the blubber of a living whale. In theory, workers would recover the dart if and when the whale was captured and cut up. The workers hated this technique, which damaged their machinery, however, so they often failed to cooperate. Moreover, the method was limited to commercial species.

The breakthrough into modern whale research was made in several places around the world when people realized that some species were individually identifiable from markings on their bodies. Combined with extensive field observation, such documentation made possible investigation of individual whales' lives, thus shedding light on movements, social structure, longevity and behaviour in a way that was previously possible only with land animals. On the West Coast, Michael Bigg of the Pacific region of the Fisheries Research Board discovered this when he realized that researchers could recognize individuals from photographs.

The federal government's sudden concern for orcas was a byproduct of aquarium orcamania. Until the mid-1960s, the feds only heard complaints from fishermen that the orcas were eating too many fish. The Vancouver Aquarium's new orcas were not the only ones being taken from the Strait of Georgia and Puget Sound region, for the area was now the centre of a flurry of commercial catching activity, supplying orcas to aquaria across North America and beyond. Questions were being raised about the ability of the population to sustain such cropping, and legislation was passed requiring a permit. Before permits could be issued it was necessary to find out how big the population was.

Bigg makes his mark

Michael Bigg helped pioneer the identification of individual orcas. (Ellis)

In October 1973, Michael Bigg had two notches cut in the dorsal fin of an orca temporarily held captive near Victoria. The notches are still visible on K1 (Taku), part of K7 subpod, but the radio transmitter that was also fitted worked for only eight hours. The technique would clearly have worked on other whales, but Bigg soon devised a better method.

Michael Bigg was the right man to do a population study of orcas. With a couple of research degrees on seals, he was well qualified to become head of marine mammal research for the Fisheries Research Board in 1970. Although he continued his seal work, he was also asked to take a census of the orcas in Canadian waters in association with similar studies in the adjacent US. After aquarium director Murray Newman suggested a one-day census, Bigg and his associates sent 15,000 questionnaires to people living and working on the coast, asking them to record sightings on July 26, 1971. In the first census, 360 orcas were reported for British Columbia, 114 for Washington, 62 in Alaska and none in Oregon. Sixty percent of those sighted were in Puget Sound or east of Vancouver Island.

Similar results in 1972 and 1973 showed the validity of the approach. Bigg undertook more detailed studies of Johnstone Strait whales, where most orcas were reported. An orca observed with an injured dorsal fin (later nicknamed Stubbs) and other whales were recognized in the following year. Gradually Bigg and his associates evolved a standardized technique. Individual whales are photographed in black and white from the left side. The shape of the dorsal fin and any injuries, and the pattern of the adjacent saddle patch, are then used to identify the individual. Records include the time and place of all sightings and the associated whales. Increasingly, observers also make hydrophone recordings of the whales' vocalizations. As the system develops, observations by the few scientists active in this research are increasingly supplemented by the work of volunteers, who watch for orcas in their travels and submit photographs. The method has spread; in 1976 Washington state started an annual census, and Alaska is now using similar techniques.

Identifying individuals

Bigg's study of orcas, one of the first to identify individuals, had one predecessor. Together these have led to applying the same approach to other species.

In an independent discovery, Roger Payne had started to use a similar identification technique on right whales in Patagonia in 1971, a year or two ahead of Bigg's work. In 1975 Payne showed a film of his work at a conference in Indiana and fascinated Jim Darling, then a University of Victoria graduate student. Gray whales had intrigued Darling when he was a surfer at Pacific Rim National Park on Vancouver Island's west coast; in 1974 he co-published a paper showing that individual grays could be identified by the skin pigments on their backs and sides. He continued the work, identifying ninety-three individual grays between 1975 and 1981, and in 1983 earned a doctorate from the University of California (Santa Cruz) with similar studies on humpbacks in Hawaii.

Humpback flukes. (Baird)

In Glacier Bay, Alaska, individual humpbacks were documented from 1968 by fluke patterns and other pigmentation. Humpbacks are identifiable from the black and white pattern on the undersides of their tails, shown off as the flukes are raised before a dive. In the 1970s, high school teacher Charles Jurasz and his wife Virginia lived on a boat and spent the summer identifying more than sixty individual humpbacks living in southeastern Alaskan inside waters. In 1976 researchers radio tagged a humpback nicknamed Friendly Fred, which remained within 15 miles (24 km) of the tagging site for the six-day study. In 1980 Olga von Ziegesar and Beth Goodwin began photo identification of the humpbacks on their summer feeding grounds.

Matriarchs rule!

Amazing results have come from orca identification studies. First, we know the population size. Individual orcas stay in the subpods in which they are born, so subpods and pods can be named, their members listed and—over the years—a genealogy established. Contrary to expectations, a matriarch leads each pod. As research documented the distribution and behaviour of resident pods, the transients' presence with their different appearance, prey and behaviour patterns have also become clear. More recently, researchers are also documenting the offshore orcas. John Ford's acoustical work integrates closely with these population studies—it depends on knowledge of which whales are making the recorded sounds—and now contributes to our growing understanding of the evolution of different groups.

In 1987 the first popular summary of this research appeared in the publication *Killer Whales. A Study of their Identification, Genealogy and Natural History in British Columbia and Washington State.* Michael Bigg, in collaboration with Graeme Ellis and John Ford in Canada and Ken Balcomb in Washington state, presented the world's first identification guide to individual whales.

By this time Bigg had been diagnosed with cancer but fought on to complete the scientific report of his work. Graeme Ellis, one of his collaborators and colleagues, managed to get an advance copy of his study from the publisher in England and rush it to his bedside just before he died in 1990. Since his death, his colleagues have substantially updated and extended the book *Killer Whales* in a new 1994 edition, appropriately dedicated to Michael Bigg. The Center for Whale Research has now published a similar identification book for orcas in Washington state, and Craig Matkin has produced an equivalent book for Prince William Sound, Alaska.

Graeme Ellis: killer whale accountant

In Canada, if you send in a photo of an orca, it will probably end up in the files of Graeme Ellis at the Fisheries Research Station in Nanaimo. When we visited, he was busy looking at strips of black and white negatives through a low-power binocular microscope—all he needs to identify most individual orcas.

Graeme Ellis keeps track of Canada's orcas. (DAES)

Ellis is in a good position to identify orcas. He has known most of British Columbia's orcas—captive or free—personally. In Campbell River where he grew up, there was not much liking for killer whales, but when he was hired straight out of school to feed captive orcas at Pender Harbour, he became enthralled and was one of the first to swim with them. For a while he worked at Sealand and helped capture whales, but he soon became unhappy with helping put whales into captivity and went to Mexico.

In 1974 he was hired on a temporary contract to work with Michael Bigg in the field and helped to develop the photo identification method that has unravelled the social structure of the orcas. "Mike was a slogger—he had great vision, could see the big picture and go for it," remembers Ellis. For a while there was no funding for orca work, "but it had become so fascinating we couldn't let it go—for many years it was done with our own money and our own time."

A photograph of the left side of an orca provides the data to allow it to be recognized. (Morton)

Twenty years later Ellis is still at it. "Most good whale research is long-term slogging," explains Ellis. "I'm working on population dynamics and social structure, and my colleagues call me the 'killer whale accountant'." Ellis has recently worked on transients, whose behaviour patterns are quite different from the residents. "You can go thirteen to fourteen years between sightings of some transients. And we've had matches from Glacier Bay, Alaska to Monterey Bay, California."

He's also intrigued by the newly discovered offshores, but with few sightings they are hard to study. This work takes incredible patience, for as Ellis said, "It needs someone stupid enough to stare at photos for hours and hours." We talked briefly about his many other projects and the prospects of funding for the next field season. I took photographs in the sunshine outside, then went on my way, while Graeme went inside to carry on sorting the thousands of photographs it takes to track whale movements and genealogy.

Independent researchers

A few West Coast whale scientists work for government, universities or other public institutions, but whales have also attracted many dedicated scientists who work outside the establishment. By finding their own funding, they attain an independence that often allows closer contact with whales; they can live where whales are active rather than in the parent institutions' cities. They may spend time in fundraising or earning a living instead of administrative chores, teaching or travel that keep establishment scientists from more frequent contact with whales. Some independent scientists are formally qualified, though they may have started out as enthusiastic amateurs. An increasing number have trained in some other area, become captivated by whale research and developed their expertise on the job.

Senior among this distinguished group of freelance researchers is Paul Spong (formerly of the University of British Columbia and the Vancouver Aquarium), who now conducts nonintrusive land-based research from Orcalab on Hanson Island in the Johnstone Strait area. Also focussed on orcas is Ken Balcomb, who manages the Center for Whale Research on San Juan Island. Alexandra Morton has worked on orcas for years from a base at Simoom Sound on Gilford (see Chapter 10), but increasingly studies the Pacific white-sided dolphin.

At Tofino on Vancouver Island's west coast, Jim Darling works with the Friends of Clayoquot to concentrate on gray and humpback whale studies. More recently, in Alaska, Craig Matkin combines fishing with orca research, while his wife Olga von Ziegesar studies humpbacks. These researchers and others work together in friendly co-operation, maximizing the use of scarce resources.

As information and expertise focus on this region of accessible whales, new students work on graduate degrees, building on available information. At the same time, local experts undertake whale research elsewhere in the world. Jim Darling studied humpbacks in Hawaii, John Ford worked on whale acoustics in the Arctic and Bruce Mate of Oregon State University uses satellites to study pilot whale and right whale migration in the Atlantic.

Thus the primary thrust of whale research has evolved. Initially a support for—and supported by—whaling, the scientific study of dead whales at whaling stations has given way to study of living whales, first in captivity and then in the field. Now conservation needs have come to dominate funding priorities; the disinterested spirit of scientific inquiry, always present, is emerging again as a major factor. Meanwhile, as whaling fades from memory, there is new interest in its impact on whales and on its rich, diverse human story.

Center for Whale Research

The US National Marine Fisheries Service, aware of Canadian orca studies, hired Ken Balcomb in 1976 to conduct a census in Washington state waters. A marine biology graduate from the University of California, he became interested in whales when he worked as dishwasher on a boat engaged in a California whale-marking project.

Ken Balcomb of the Center for Whale Research surveys the "Orca freeway." (DAES)

Ken and associates took 14,000 photographs, and his study confirmed Bigg's results. Although government funding ran out after seven months, more than two decades later Ken still works on whales. His hangout is on Smugglers Cove on San Juan Island. The Center for Whale Research is a house on a cliff, with a deck-mounted telescope overlooking a spectacular view of the orcas' main highway past the islands. Its furnishing is eclectic—I have never before seen a grand piano decorated with an orca skull, which Ken bought for $500 on tour in Japan with the US Navy.

The Center operates two boats and finds whales by networking with whale watching operators. It assists with many specialized research projects, including a DNA biopsy study and measurements of pesticide residues in fat. With an Environmental Education grant, they are also developing educational kits. After twenty years of dedicated work, Balcomb has not run out of projects. "I'm doing what I want to do. I want to expand the techniques: I don't want to use the whales as guinea pigs. After all, they are the king of beasts."

Apart from occasional grants, support comes from regular volunteers such as Astrid von Ginneken, a Rotterdam medical researcher who pays her way over every summer to work on the project. Since 1987 changing teams of Earthwatch volunteers have come from around the world, contributing funds for the privilege of giving time to the project.

"It's one way to work in a holiday frame of mind, yet do something useful and constructive," said Australian volunteer David Higgs. "Volunteers arrive on a Sunday which is spent in a briefing, getting to know one another and sorting out accommodation." On the second day they learn to use the photographic methods and research boats. Then they spend time out in the boats photographing whales, observing them through the telescopes, writing up the records and maintaining the files containing thousands of photos, not of "mug shots" but of "fin shots" which document orcas. "In the last few years more than a thousand Earthwatch volunteers have gone through the Orca Survey," Balcomb said. "Killer whales are the most charismatic animals. People feel they are witnessing such amazing creatures."

Orca takes all

In Victoria, Robin Baird and associates were gathering data on strandings and studying the feeding habits of transient orcas. One day Baird attempted to pick up parts of a harbor porpoise killed by a transient orca to test for pesticides and genetic data. After two attempts with the orca still around, he netted the parts, but before he could pull the net out the orca came and grabbed the lot. Baird later commented: "I was left holding the extension handle and nothing else. I was very surprised!"

Rod Palm

Rod Palm of Strawberry Island Research studies transient orcas and other wildlife. A former marine historian and archaeologist, Rod has lived for twenty-five years on the first Vancouver ferry, now high and dry on Strawberry Island near Tofino. He also runs whale watching tours and has persuaded other whale watching outfits in the region to contribute a dollar a head to whale research programs.

Joan Goddard: Whaling historian

As you enter her quiet suburban home in Victoria, you would not immediately guess that Joan Goddard is a passionate pursuer of whaling history. A clock mounted in a sperm whale tooth gives the first clue. In the nearby study are shelves stacked high with books on whaling and a computer she uses to access the marine mammal research and conservation group on the Internet. With a degree in natural sciences, Joan is quick to point out that she is not a professional historian. That has not stopped her from becoming an expert on many aspects of BC whaling history and a guest curator at the Maritime Museum of British Columbia.

Joan Goddard, descendant of BC whalers, has brought many of their stories to light. (DAES)

"It was the whale's tooth that did it," she wrote. A treasure of her mother's childhood made her realize how little she had known about that period of her family's lives. Joan Goddard's grandfather, William Rolls, from an old Newfoundland mercantile family, worked for the Pacific Whaling Company. At first he was the bookkeeper at Sechart, and between 1913 and 1933 he managed Rose Harbour and Naden Harbour stations in the Queen Charlotte Islands. Consequently, her mother spent summers on the stations and eventually married a Swedish logger. Joan grew up with whale souvenirs and old photo albums, but took no real interest in the unusual family history until her mother was aging.

Living in Oregon, Joan brought her sailboat to British Columbia waters every summer; in 1981 she circumnavigated Vancouver Island. At Clayoquot she found artifacts from the old whaling station, but the Sechart plant was not even on the charts. Her mother gave her the names of children in the faded photos. Joan used British Columbia phone books to find descendants of five families, including those of an English steam engineer, station managers recruited from Newfoundland and a Japanese crew foreman. (Chinese who worked at the station were not allowed to bring out wives.) In 1982 Joan organized a reunion of the children of the whaling station—the first time most of them had met for seventy years. "I found three who had been the engineer's sons, one of the Japanese sons, and the manager's daughter who had all played together in 1916," Joan remembers. "It was pandemonium; they were all excited and reminiscing."

Opposite: Rod Palm, (at the wheel) an independent whale researcher based in Tofino, with the author. (AJS)

Gradually Joan found herself on the speaking circuit and writing more pieces about British Columbia whaling history, culminating in her book *A Window on Whaling in British Columbia.* Her research has extended to aboriginal whaling; she travels regularly to meetings in the eastern USA and has attended a whaling history conference in Norway. Her interests focus on the future as well as the past. "I would like to write about how we are going to relate to whales in the next century—about use of whales with respect."

Whales for Tomorrow

A pair of adult male killer whales cruise the Pacific Ocean off SE Alaska. (Baird)

In 1959 the Canadian Department of Fisheries and Oceans mounted a machine gun above Seymour Narrows, a narrow stretch of water between Vancouver Island and the much smaller Quadra Island. The gun was to be fired at passing killer whales—as they were invariably called then—to reduce the population to levels acceptable to fishermen in the nearby resort town of Campbell River. In the end the machine gun was never fired. Nevertheless, many fishermen and others shot at orcas; a quarter of the orcas later captured for aquaria had bullet wounds. Imagine public response if the government set up a gun today!

In the environmentally conscious 1990s, it is difficult to remember—or imagine—that in the early 1960s most people were scarcely aware of whales. If they gave large whales any thought, it was as so much meat on the move. Killer whales were widely regarded as the most dangerous animals in the sea, liable to attack anything from helpless swimmers to great whales. Most people had no more affection for them than for sharks. No public protest arose when whalers sailed from Coal Harbour, or when navy fighter planes used orcas for target practice.

In 1975, Mike Bailey of Greenpeace placed himself between a catcher and a whale, providing a photo op that brought whaling to attention worldwide. (Weyler)

Yet we had been changing our views of and relationship to cetacea for some time. Even in the mid-nineteenth century, some whalers themselves expressed concern at their prey's rapid disappearance; the twentieth century brought increasingly strenuous efforts to outlaw whaling altogether. Living whales at last seem a greater asset than dead ones; the area where the machine gun was set up is now an active centre of our multimillion-dollar whale watching industry.

Controlling whaling

Whaling history records the headlong destruction of successive species and populations of large whales until hunting them is no longer economical; they have reached what is termed "commercial extinction." As whalers improved ship capacity and range and developed new technology for slaughtering and processing carcasses, they hunted large whales—right, sperm and gray whales, then the large rorquals—to near extinction. But whalers are highly capitalized and always lose interest in species before the last whale is dead; even a heavily exploited species has at least a theoretical chance of recovery.

Whalers have usually known the consequences of their actions for the whales they hunted. One whaler wrote in 1845, "The poor whale is doomed to utter extermination, or at least, so near to it that too few will remain to tempt the cupidity of man...In view of the destruction which has been made...we may safely suppose another century will witness the entire abandonment of the fishery, from a scarcity of whales."

Awareness has not stayed the whalers' hands; whales not taken by one nation have usually fallen prey to another. No one country can manage an international resource. Conservation of whales in the open oceans is possible only through development of mechanisms for sharing international responsibility.

Models for successful co-operation do exist. The 1911 fur seal treaty—signed by Great Britain (for Canada), Japan, Russia and the United States—allocated seals amicably between signatories and protected the seals of Alaska's Pribilof Islands.

First attempts at international co-operation to protect whales proved far less successful. Despite the decline of some whale species, the total catch rose and rose until between 1930 and 1940, whalers captured 2.5 to 3 million tons (2.3 to 2.7 million tonnes) of whales each year. In 1938 whalers took 55,000 whales and recorded the maximum tonnage. In later years they took more individual whales but lower tonnage because they took younger whales.

International Whaling Commission

After earlier efforts, the International Convention for the Regulation of Whaling was set up in 1946, focussing on conservation of whale stocks so whalers could continue to "crop" them. Its management body, the International Whaling Commission (IWC), first met in 1948. Canada—then whaling actively on both coasts—signed the convention in 1946. By 1947 seventeen nations had signed. Canada attended the first meeting and made the convention Canadian law with the Whaling Convention Act (1951). The IWC was supposed to scientifically determine whaling quotas that would protect and rebuild whale stocks, safeguard future breeding stocks, set up sanctuaries to protect breeding areas and protect endangered species. In practice, it became a whalers' club which made token gestures toward setting quotas but allowed each member to take any whales they wanted on the high seas. There was no means of policing or enforcing the voluntary agreements.

In 1972 the United Nations Conference on the Human Environment recommended a ten-year moratorium on whaling, which the IWC rejected. The next decade was politically complex. Nonwhaling nations joined the commission and voted against whaling, whaling nations withdrew or found loopholes and non-members continued "pirate" whaling.

Initially, the US backed the moratorium and imposed trade sanctions on countries that ignored IWC quotas. In the late 1970s, however, after whaling nations outflanked the USA on the aboriginal whaling issue, US support for the ban faded. In 1980 Canada's delegation objected to the proposed moratorium and unexpectedly voted with the whalers; the resulting uproar at home led Canada (no longer a whaling nation) to drop out of the IWC altogether in 1981.

IWC quotas dropped below 40,000 in 1974, to 30,000 in 1976, to 20,000 in 1979 and to 10,000 in 1983. By 1985 the quota was zero—essentially reflecting belated acceptance of the moratorium.

Only Norway and Japan objected to the zero quota, and both countries continued to take Minke whales for "research." World public opinion had affected member and nonmember nations alike, and a major force influencing public opinion worldwide originated in Vancouver.

Greenpeace leads the way

The international conservation organization Greenpeace began in Vancouver, initially as a loose group of rather mystical hippie war protestors, ecology grad students and radical journalists. In 1971 Greenpeace sailed on an ancient halibut seiner to publicly oppose American nuclear testing at Amchitka in the Aleutians. On the way, members visited the abandoned Akutan whaling station and collected giant bones as souvenirs. It was a moment of truth. "We had been so intent on trying to prevent a holocaust, we had forgotten that for this other race of giant creatures the holocaust had already come," said Robert Hunter later. On the return voyage they saw large whales, one of which dived under the boat.

Paul Spong joined the group after his controversial departure

The crews of the Greenpeace vessel James Bay *and a Russian catcher shared a keen interest in whales, but nothing else. (Weyler)*

from his Vancouver Aquarium research position (see Chapter 7). He was already "a bit of a legend among eco-freaks on the West Coast" after his stand for freedom of the aquarium orcas. In 1973 he stimulated a new direction in the organization, shifting some of its efforts toward protecting great whales. A meeting with Canadian author Farley Mowat, coincidentally touring to promote his book *A Whale for the Killing*, led to development of a national strategy to end Canadian whaling. Fundraising by the Greenpeace Christmas Whale Show and help from singer Gordon Lightfoot allowed Spong to take a protest to Japan in 1974. He was hospitably received, and his live presentations and television appearances reached some 30,000 people—yet ultimately he felt he had made little impact.

Too big an ocean?

Greenpeace's next step was to intervene directly in commercial whaling, drawing public attention to the UN moratorium request. An advisor told them that they had no chance—"it's too big an ocean." But fuelled by Cree prophesies, the I Ching and other New Age inspiration, the Vancouver group gathered an even more diverse volunteer crew and readied their ship *Greenpeace V*, using a Kwakwa'ka'wakw (Kwakiutl) killer-whale crest as its symbol.

The expedition's huge sendoff at Jericho Beach in April 1975 caught worldwide media attention.

Meanwhile, Spong travelled to Scandinavia and used his scientific contacts to acquire information about previous kill areas—and learned that whaling was unlikely for several months. The expedition filled in time while trying to remain newsworthy. Paul Watson, a leader, had an appendix operation while the ship called in at former whaling station Coal Harbour to seek information from retired whalers and introduced members to gray whales off Tofino. Musicians serenaded whales from Zodiacs; one came close enough to demonstrate its bad case of halitosis.

Greenpeace members intervene in Russian whaling in a dramatic confrontation, 1975. (Weyler)

On the day that the IWC began its meeting in London, Greenpeace encountered Russian whalers on the high seas off California and documented them killing immature whales. In a dramatic intervention, volunteers in Zodiacs manoeuvred between a catcher boat and its prey. "I heard the sound of the harpoon going off and the 'whish' of the cable whipping out behind it," reported Hunter. "It slashed the water less than five feet from the port side of our rubber boat." The resulting film footage went around the world.

Greenpeace achieved its goal of raising public consciousness about whales and whaling, and a secondary benefit soon became apparent—the development of ad hoc Greenpeace groups across North America and a mailing list of 10,000 supporters. So began the laborious process of converting a loose, rather flaky group into an efficient worldwide conservation organization that could sustain its dynamic visionary approach.

Actions against the Russian fleet continued in 1976; the

Japanese fleet pulled back to avoid confrontation. The following year, Greenpeace was active in Pacific and Australian waters, stimulating formation of a Royal Commission on whaling policy which led to a total Australian ban on whaling on scientific and ethical grounds. In 1978 another Greenpeace vessel was active in the Atlantic. Later protests in support of whales took place ashore in Japan, Iceland, Norway, New Zealand and the United Kingdom. In 1988 Greenpeace received a United Nations Environmental Program award for "outstanding environmental achievement." At its peak in 1990, the organization had offices in 32 countries and a membership of 4.8 million people; in 1997 it still had nearly 3 million.

Should we keep whales in captivity?

Haida was the star of Sealand in Oak Bay, putting on shows every day. (DAES)

Dolphins and other small whales were kept in aquaria for four decades without serious opposition before controversy erupted over the capture of the first orcas. Ironically, until orcas were seen in aquaria, most people regarded them as fierce, dangerous and detrimental to fisheries. People gained new perspectives largely from aquarium exhibitions and capture-related research. When orcas first seemed apparently harmless giant dolphins doing tricks, then highly intelligent family-oriented fish-eating mammals, many people questioned the appropriateness of keeping such animals in captivity. Eventually, controversy surrounded most aspects of captivity: methods and locations of capture, appropriate care of captive orcas, and whether and how to release captive whales.

Those who favour exhibition—a majority in North America, according to 1990s polls—point out that aquaria conduct important research and educate millions of people who would never see cetaceans in the wild. Aquaria also occasionally save injured whales unable to survive in the wild, such as the sick and injured Miracle who survived four years at Sealand.

Murray Newman: Appreciate and protect

Murray Newman was director of the Vancouver Aquarium for thirty-seven years, through the controversial period when orcas first became part of the aquarium business. His autobiography *Life in a Fishbowl* offers insights from the aquarium perspective. Initially there was no cause to anticipate public concern about orcas, he wrote. "Marine mammals were either being slaughtered for business or killed as pests...Why couldn't our society appreciate and protect these animals?"

Murray Newman was director of the Vancouver Aquarium when it took a world lead in orca display. (Hua)

Education was a strong motivation, and at first the aquarium presented "whale shows." Newman claimed that "Skana seemed to enjoy performing before an audience." He acknowledged orcas as the biggest reason for the aquarium's expansion and recognized the three-fold dilemma that "they need as much space as you can give them," that this takes dollars and that the many visitors they attract require an infrastructure to serve their needs. Over the years, Newman and his board and staff raised funds to provide ever bigger orca pools and replaced whale performances with interpretation emphasizing their natural behaviour and environment.

Newman faced much active opposition and recognized that "keeping killer whales in captivity is most certainly a moral issue." His strongest argument, however, was that "Without aquariums, the plight of killer whales would be as ignored as that of moose in the forests of British Columbia." History seems to support his view.

Aquaria draw several criticisms: captive whales should not have to perform like circus animals; only whales bred in captivity should be in aquaria (i.e., no further capture of wild whales); and whales in captivity should breed only in facilities adequate for raising live young. Some people feel that there is no need to show larger species in captivity; others feel that no whales of any kind should be held captive. The Canadian Zoo and Aquarium Association has recently adopted a policy that wild animals should not be kept in captivity for purely commercial or recreational purposes.

Increasingly, municipalities forbid captive animals other than familiar pets. In 1996 the Vancouver Parks Board directed the Vancouver Aquarium to find ways of phasing out its captive whales.

Several experienced scientists and conservationists support releasing individual captive whales, partly on ethical grounds and partly to find out if whales would be accepted back by their own pods.

"It's not their role to be our slaves for entertainment and cash flow," said Ken Balcomb. Animal rights activists express similar views. Peter Hamilton, who has actively campaigned for the release of captive orcas, is among the most outspoken.

Peter Hamilton: Freedom not captivity

Peter Hamilton works through the Lifeforce Foundation in Vancouver. In his book *Orca: A Family Story*, he wrote that in 1982 he used ultralight aircraft to stop Sealand of the Pacific from capturing a killer whale family in Pedder Bay near Victoria, and that in 1992 he and others succeeded in shutting down Sealand of the Pacific. Introduced as a "fictional story," it nevertheless gave dates and details of the 1968 capture of A5 pod in Pender Harbour. The fictional element appears to be speculation on future release of West Coast orcas in US aquaria at the time he wrote the book.

Using such emotive terms as "cruelly imprisoned," "marine mammal slave trade," and "victims of the aquarium entertainment industry," Hamilton wrote of captured whales that die before reaching aquaria or survive only briefly in captivity. He also criticized orca performances and advertising which give "irresponsible portrayals of wildlife."

"The animal trade also exemplifies speciesism human tyranny over other sentient creatures with whom we share this planet," he wrote. He also documented closures of marine aquaria around the world, successful releases of cetaceans to the wild and UK plans to create a virtual reality "animal free zoo."

Haida lobtails for the customers, providing entertainment with natural behaviour. (DAES)

Freeing Willy

Keiko, star of the *Free Willy* movies which feature orcas escaping from captivity, may be our best-known captive orca. People noted the irony that Keiko—captured near Iceland in the 1980s—remained for years in a Mexico City theme park. A triangular public relations battle soon raged over Keiko. On one side, the Free Willy Foundation (a consortium of interested organizations) was trying to secure his release, advised by whale scientists including Jim Darling. In the middle, his owners El Nuevo Reino Aventura were apparently open-minded. On the other side, the Alliance of Marine Parks and Aquariums, representing thirty-two agencies with the most to lose from Keiko's release, quickly outflanked opponents by funding improvements to Keiko's theme park habitat.

In January 1996, Keiko moved to a new $7-million tank in Newport, Oregon, to refamiliarize him with a wild environment and allow eventual release. Warner Brothers, which made the movies, contributed to the cost, but more than $400 million came from North American children and their families responding to an emotional appeal on *Free Willy* videotapes. In his new tank, Keiko's weight increased, his health improved and his breath retention rose from three to twenty minutes.

In September 1998, Keiko was shifted to another facility in Iceland, where he can communicate with local orcas. "It's quite possible that he won't be released," said Diane Hammond of the Free Willy Keiko Foundation. "We're not going to make that decision until we really know whether he can succeed or not."

In the early 1990s, Paul Spong pointed out a better candidate for release. Corky—her stage name is Shamu—in San Diego's Sea World was captured in 1969. Since Corky still speaks her local dialect and researchers know her pod, she has a better chance of successful readaptation than Keiko.

How many whales?

As the world's aquaria recognized the Pacific Northwest as a source of accessible orcas, Ted Griffin of the Seattle Aquarium and Bob Wright of Sealand captured many whales. By 1972 Griffin and others had taken some sixty orcas for seventeen different aquaria.

A bigger player in the orca capture business was Don Goldsberry of Sea World, whose March 1976 masterpiece of bad timing accelerated the rate and effectiveness of orca protection. Goldsberry was using aircraft and seal bombs to herd a Puget Sound pod past the state legislature, where representatives were debating a Puget Sound Orca Sanctuary, into Budd Inlet. At nearby Evergreen State College, where a three-day orca conference was in progress, scientists took a strong interest in the event. More than a thousand people visited the capture site, and although a case against Goldsberry was dismissed, he lost his permit.

By this time, Bigg had completed his population studies (see Chapter 7), and it was clear that large numbers of orcas were being taken from a population of fewer than 350. In 1976 Bigg formally presented his findings with Allen Wolman. "In British Columbia and Washington 263 killer whales...were caught during 1962–73 of which 50 were kept for oceanaria... Revenue to be netted from the sale of 48 killer whales is estimated to be about $1,000,000." The two scientists recommended that no more orcas be taken from the region except to replace animals that died in Canadian aquaria.

Laws and conventions

A blue whale shows its flukes, free to move through the seas since the moratorium on whaling took effect in 1985. (Baird)

In 1972 the US enacted its Marine Mammal Protection Act to prohibit Americans from taking marine mammals and to refuse entry of marine mammals or their products into the United States. Exception was made for aboriginal hunting, such as Alaska Natives' subsistence hunt for the bowhead whale. In 1973 the US established the Convention on International Trade in Endangered Species, which led to the 1973 US Endangered Species Act giving additional protection to listed whale species. A revised US Marine Mammal Protection Act in 1994, however, reduced government control over cetaceans in captivity.

The bowhead whale was the first cetacean listed by the Committee on the Status of Endangered Species in Canada (COSEWIC). This designation has no legal status, however, but is merely a recommendation for action by the Federal Department of Fisheries and Oceans, the agency responsible for marine mammals. In 1998 Canada drafted an Endangered Species Act, but it died when the election was called. A proposed private members' bill had little chance of success.

Endangered whales

Pacific Northwest whale species listed by the World Wildlife Fund, with estimates of current populations:

right whale—120 animals in north Pacific in 1991 after 50 years of protection; 15 sightings in 50 years
blue—may be fewer than 1,000 worldwide
humpback—northeastern Pacific population of about 2,000
sei—10,000 in north Pacific
gray—16,500 in eastern Pacific
fin—200,000 worldwide
sperm—world population 700,000 to 2,000,000

In 1976 the US Fisheries Conservation Management Act extended an exclusive fishing zone 200 miles (321 km) from the coast; non-US whalers were prohibited except under permit. Canada followed suit in 1977 with a limit of 200 nautical miles (370 km).

Fisheries Act regulations allow fines up to $100,000 for disturbing marine mammals. First Peoples are allowed to hunt (without a licence) all cetaceans except right whales for local consumption. Amendments in 1994 to the US Marine Mammal Protection Act permitted Alaskan Natives to set up co-management agreements with federal agencies, giving them an equal role in managing marine mammals.

Protecting wild whales

If people stop killing whales, need we worry about them in the wild? If no whales should be kept in aquaria—as some people feel—can we go and watch them swimming in their natural habitat?

This gray whale is caught up in fishing gear off Vancouver Island. (Baird)

As so often in nature, the answers are complex.

Even without human disturbance, the wild waters have their own hazards. Whales may be trapped in ice or stranded on land. For millions of years, whales have coped with sickness, parasitic infections, accidental injury and food shortages. Since our species came along to complicate their lives—even if we no longer deliberately kill or capture them—whales have also suffered multiple human impacts including accidental death through commercial fishing, collisions with ships, competition for food and a host of more subtle, possibly more deadly, cumulative effects of disturbance and pollution.

Stranded whales

In June 1979 a large herd of sperm whales stranded themselves on the beach at Florence, Oregon. Fortunately, the Society of American mammalogists was meeting nearby and documented the event.

Stranding is a great puzzle of whale behaviour. Individuals and sometimes large groups run themselves on shore, where—in the normal course of events—they usually die. Individual strandings of any species are often of dead or sick whales no longer in control of their destiny; mass strandings are usually of a few species of deep-water toothed whales with little experience of shallow water.

Some strandings occur where geography and a great tide fall combine to create a "whale trap." Whale sonar may be less effective where water is shallowing or when there is storm noise. Other possible explanations include a parasite that may impair hearing and a sensitivity to fluctuations in the earth's magnetic field that may mislead migrating whales. Mass strandings may result from whales' strong social character, encouraging them to stay together even as a leader runs them into some form of danger. Stranded whales undergo physiological changes which lead them to become thirsty, drink seawater and die of salt poisoning. As their circulation systems fail, toxins accumulate in their bodies.

Whale strandings often alarm humans, who struggle to return smaller whales to the sea. Some stay clear; many run themselves ashore again. Returning stranded whales to the ocean may not be wholly beneficial, apart from the practical difficulties, for several reasons.

Sick whales could reintroduce diseases, endangering wild whales. Rescue is not crucial to the survival of most whales prone to mass stranding, since these species are relatively common. Humane euthanasia can spare the whale further suffering in the later stages of a stranding, though humans may find this difficult.

Human observers—focussing full attention on the whale—may suffer from hypothermia. And now that whaling has essentially ended, strandings are the only source of biological material for research into breeding, population dynamics and genetics of species not easily observed in the wild. Report a stranding as soon as possible to the nearest marine biological station, whale museum or aquarium.

Sweeping the ocean

Drift nets created a special hazard for whales until they were outlawed. North Pacific fishermen set nets for tuna and squid for half of every year. The nets were 50 feet (15 m) deep and stretched 30,000 to 45,000 miles (48,000 to72,000 km) in total. Set at night and sometimes left for days, they made large "incidental" catches of other fish, including salmon, and many whales. Since echolocation could not easily detect the fine monofilament lines, many whales—particularly small toothed whales—drowned. Some nets got loose and drifted free, continuing to kill until they sank under the weight of bodies. An estimated 40,000 Dall's porpoises died in the north Pacific every year.

At first it was hard to gather objective statistics. Japanese, Taiwanese and other fishermen using these nets resisted international observers on their fish boats. Seeking accurate figures, in

1986–87 the Canadian fisheries department tested squid drift nets on two vessels and found that they killed 135 dolphins, porpoises and other small whales. Canada consequently banned drift net fishing in Canadian waters. Drift nets are now outlawed internationally, but some may still be used illegally. The best deterrent to this wasteful fishing is for consumers to buy only "dolphin friendly" tuna. Look for cans with a logo indicating that the tuna was taken without endangering dolphins.

Is watching whales harmless to them? There is increasing concern about, but little research on, the impact of whale watching on wild populations. (Baird)

Whale harassment

A couple of centuries ago, a pod of orcas could travel in peace, meeting only an occasional First Nations canoe or a small sailing ship. By contrast, on July 28, 1995, J, K and L pods travelled together as a superpod past Lime Kiln Park on San Juan Island—accompanied by thirty-five kayaks and sixty boats! Kayaks are silent, but any boat under power makes a noise that may disturb a species which navigates—and finds its food—by echolocation.

Greatly increased commercial traffic in the inland waters of Puget Sound and the Strait of Georgia makes for inevitable contact between whales and vessels. Now that orcas are under close examination, researchers find that many whales bear possible propeller scars.

As recreational boating increases and interest in all whale species grows, boats are likely to follow or intercept any slow-moving individual or pod travelling in busy waters. I have even observed planes landing to watch whales pass. Some boaters are so fascinated or careless that they go close enough to disturb the whales, even rushing through the middle of a pod. This causes particular concern when unusual species appear or return to a former habitat. In May 1995, for instance, three gray whales heading past Sidney near Victoria were surrounded by a flurry of small boats. One whale was reportedly injured by a propeller, and fisheries officer Bob MacDonald had to warn boaters to keep their distance.

The many responsible and understanding observers have little individual impact, but the cumulative effect can amount to serious harassment. Many who feel that whales should not be kept captive suggest that the public can unobtrusively enjoy whales by whale watching. But is it possible that the growing whale watching industry itself is adversely affecting whales, as more boats head out more often specifically to contact and follow gray whales and orcas? Increasingly, governments are developing behaviour guidelines for boat captains in the presence of whales. Voluntary whale watching industry associations also encourage members to act responsibly. When you travel with a reputable captain or see passing boats respectfully stop their engines to watch, it seems unlikely the whales would be much disturbed. Yet everyone has stories of a fish boat—or even a whale watcher's Zodiac—that charges into the middle of a resting pod and sends them all below.

How could anyone tell if boats disturb whales? Charles and Virginia Jurasz, observing humpbacks in Glacier Bay, have noted evidence that whales avoid the increased boat traffic, including large liners. But other than a general impression, how do we know if boaters are harassing whales? Can we measure the amount of disturbance that significantly affects their lives? Research on this problem started as long ago as 1983 with a study in the Johnstone Strait. Susan Krause of the University of California observed from high ground on West Cracroft Island to avoid disturbing the whales herself. She used a theodolite to make careful observations of both orca pods and boats. With several thousands of observations over the summer, she was able to compare the behaviour of undisturbed whales, which swam at an average 8.65 miles per hour (5.19 kph) through the day, with those close to boats, which swam nearly half again as fast and fastest when the most boats were near. As whales become accustomed to the presence of watchers there may be less effect; more recent research has shown that vessels keeping the regulation distance of 300 feet (100 m) have little impact.

Marine parks

On the last day of his presidency in 1913, William Taft signed an order protecting fish and wildlife throughout the Aleutian Islands. No one consulted the Alaska Whaling Company owners, who had just built the Akutan whaling station. Horrified, they lobbied the Department of Lands without success. Eventually they persuaded Woodrow Wilson, the succeeding president, to order an amendment to allow whaling.

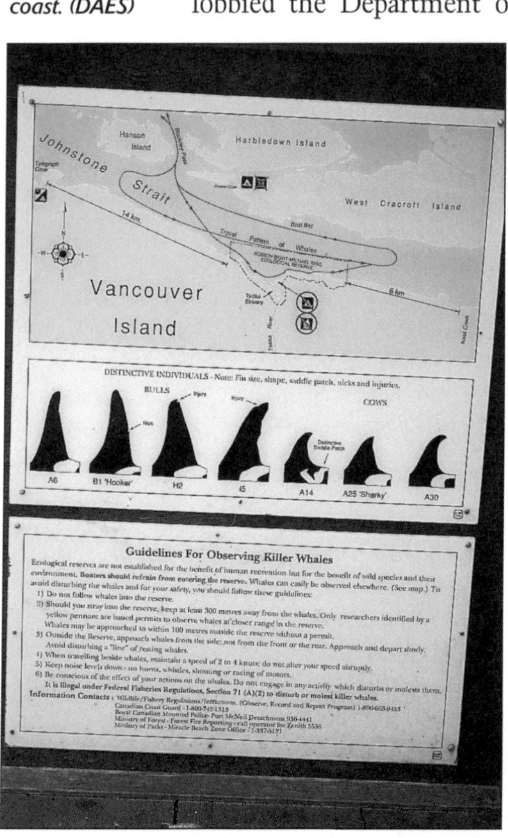

Robson Bight/Michael Bigg Ecological Reserve information sign is mounted in Telegraph Cove, source of many whale watching trips along the coast. (DAES)

Marine parks that would actually protect whales were a long time coming; researchers can find it hard to pinpoint specific vitally important areas for wide-ranging species. One such area is in Robson Bight in Johnstone Strait east of Vancouver Island. Here orcas gather almost every day in summer and rub their bodies on the pebbly beaches. Although this intriguing and unusual behaviour has been known since the 1960s, conservation interest at first lay only in fish; the adjacent Tsitika River was the last untouched watershed on the east coast of Vancouver Island and thus an important salmon habitat. In 1973 the British Columbia government had declared a moratorium on logging and road building there, but by the 1980s the forest giant MacMillan Bloedel seemed likely to log the area and create a log dump where the whales gathered.

Strenuous efforts by a small group of whale enthusiasts—including writer Erich Hoyt, and Jim Borrowman and Bill MacKay of Telegraph Cove, assisted by a small band of researchers—averted the disaster. In 1982 the government set aside a sea area of 3,089 acres (1,248 ha) and an adjacent land area of 1,250 acres (505 ha) as the Robson Bight Ecological Reserve. In 1991 the name of

Michael Bigg was added in honour of the whale researcher. Boats are not allowed in the reserve, where staff and a team of volunteer wardens monitor each summer.

Canada's Oceans Act, proclaimed in 1997, and a proposed Marine Conservation Areas Act will give legislative backing for a network of marine protection areas, with a possible pilot in the Southern Gulf Islands.

Bruce Patterson: Park volunteer

When we met Bruce on the dock at Telegraph Cove, he had just completed three months as a volunteer warden for the Michael Bigg reserve and was on his way home to Switzerland. Originally an English immunologist, he got frustrated with the shortage of research funding and became a drilling engineer in the oil industry, working all over in the world. He now works six months of the year, then travels to watch wildlife.

Bruce Patterson, a park volunteer. (DAES)

He had taken a summer of camping in his stride and spent his days watching whale watchers and patrolling the edge of the restricted waters in a Zodiac. The team worked in all weather except the roughest. "It's more important to educate people than introduce laws that can't be enforced," said Bruce. "Ninety-five percent of the people stay out of the reserve—it's more of a problem when people get too close to whales." Certainly he has observed people harassing whales, for example, float planes landing in the middle of a pod.

His reward is living with the whales. "One day we saw ninety-three," he remembered, "and one day one breached a metre from the boat."

Most memorable was a night when dinoflagellates (microscopic algae) had created bioluminescence—a natural light in the water. "I was drifting in a canoe, when an orca swam underneath, and the water lit up bright green." How did the orca experience stack up with Bruce's other travels? "It's as good as anything I've done—equal with Africa."

Robson Bight is the only ecological reserve specifically for whales, but other protected marine areas exist. British Columbia's Pacific Rim National Park and Gwaii Haanas South Moresby National Marine Park Reserves include marine sections, though the province's marine park system focusses more on recreation than conservation. The 2,500 square nautical miles of the Olympic Coast National Marine Sanctuary, off 135 miles (217 km) of Washington state's Olympic Peninsula, offers protection to gray and other whales.

Hints of a gradual return of grays and humpbacks to sheltered waters and their ensuing disturbance suggest that we may need other reserves. People for Puget Sound is one organization gathering support for a Northwest Straits Marine Sanctuary which will ban oil pipelines and supertanker ports. Canada's Parks and Wilderness Society (CPAWS) leads attempts to develop a National Marine Conservation Area in the Southern Gulf Islands.

Mercury and PCBs

Whales venturing into sheltered waters have more to worry about than boater harassment. Four pulp mills surround British Columbia's inland waters; others operate in Washington state. The area also receives waste waters from a population of several million. Despite increasing concern about the quality of our near-shore water, levels of some poisons have only just started to decline. Poisonous chemicals and oil can poison the water and work up the food chain to cetaceans, while abundant sewage and other organic materials encourage algal blooms which produce their own toxins. Widely travelled whale species may bring in poisons from other areas, but whales that do not travel far are more likely to pick up poisons locally. Data show little impact on whales, but there is enough to raise some concerns. Extensive study of the ecological impact of the 1989 *Exxon Valdez* oil spill

Pulp mills surround sheltered waters, and have been blamed for pollution that travels up the food chain. (DAES)

showed that thirteen of thirty-five resident orcas of Prince William Sound had disappeared by 1990. The Marine Mammal Research Group established the Stranded Whale and Dolphin Program (SWDP) in 1987 with a mandate to sample tissues of dead whales for pollutants. In 1987 observers reported twenty-four strandings, followed by twenty-eight in 1988. One specimen, a false killer whale stranded on Denman Island, contained "very high levels of pesticides and heavy metals, including the highest level of liver mercury ever recorded for cetaceans." Orcas and gray whales also contain dioxins and PCBs.

We will be going whaling again

Since worldwide whaling has almost stopped, and public interest in cetaceans runs at an all-time high, we could easily assume that the future is bright for our cetaceans. The cessation of whaling is formally an annually renewed ten-year moratorium, however, while stocks are properly counted and sustainable quotas established. And aboriginal whaling is not a lost art. "We will be going whaling again," said a Nuu-chah-nulth spokesman.

The Makah of the Olympic west coast regard whaling as an important part of their identity as a people. In their 1855 treaty with the US government, they retained the right to take whales. The International Whaling Commission has now also given permission. In 1995 the Makah applied to the US National Marine Service for a permit to take whales, which they received in 1998. In November they set sail in a storm of rumour and controversy. The Makah, who hurled harpoons from dugout canoes in their ancient style, pointed out that their hunt is rooted in tradition. For humanitarian reasons the commission insisted, however, that the hunters must dispatch a harpooned whale with a machine gun. Makah whaling has the support of other First Nations, some of whom travelled to Neah Bay for a potlatch. Leader Tom Mexsis Happynook, hereditary whaling chief of the related Nuu-chah-nulth, is also president of the Victoria-based World Council of Whalers, which supports aboriginal and subsistence whaling around the world. Local whale watching companies are concerned that their trade will suffer. The Victoria-based Westcoast Anti-Whaling Society and Seattle's Project Sea Wolf held public meetings opposing the hunt and mounted a flotilla of boats—including Paul Watson's *Sea Shepherd III*—to picket ferries and follow the Makah on their hunt. They broadcast orca calls from a submarine painted to simulate an orca to scare grays away and videotape the kill. As excitement mounted, more than 100 reporters camped out in Neah Bay.

Protestors have also used US freedom of information legislation to acquire documents such as a 1995 memo in which the Makah mention plans for a processing plant—to process whales taken by other aboriginal groups—and their approaches to Japanese and Norwegian markets.

As October dragged on, bad weather delayed the hunt and frayed tempers. In November protestors landed on the reserve, supported by some Makah members who oppose the hunt, and tribal police arrested four. Other protests have been less focussed. A Victoria bumper sticker said, "Save the whales—harpoon a Makah."

A future for whales?

Within the ocean, whale species are in a perpetually shifting balance with the abundance of their prey. As plankton, squid and fish numbers rise and fall, so do whale numbers. Seals and larger fish, their wild competitors for the same food sources, also shift in numbers accordingly. This constantly adjusting balance in the sea has evolved since life first appeared. In recent centuries, it has been increasingly skewed by the heavy-handed interventions of another mammal species, one capable of catching multitudes of fish, pursuing living whales, building ships, designing exploding harpoons and exploiting all of the ocean's resources from plankton to great whales.

No longer can the underwater world look after itself; its survival depends upon the action—or inaction—of humans. North Americans have mismanaged the major fish stocks on which we ourselves depend, such as the Atlantic cod and now the west coast salmon. By our actions, we have co-opted the responsibility of life-and-death decisions for whales. How can we protect whales when we have made such a mess of the fisheries which support both whales and people?

Large and conspicuous animals need abundant food. The largest baleen whales depend mostly on huge quantities of relatively tiny plankton—a blue whale eats 3 tons (3 tonnes) of krill per day. Our rapidly increasing world population has sparked some attempts to bypass whales and harvest krill directly. Krill is reportedly not very tasty, but it can supply abundant calories to a hungry horde.

The little Minke —despised by earlier whalers — is the only whale still hunted commercially. (Baird)

The sperm whale and many smaller toothed whales depend on squid, now being fished in huge quantities with no attempt to assess environmental impact. Smaller whales of inshore waters also depend on getting their share of the region's fish—from salmon to small schooling species—all of which are now dwindling alarmingly for reasons that are not always clear. Orca populations have remained more or less static since we started keeping records—so we can't blame the whales for fish losses. But scientists report an apparent thinning of blubber—an indication of poor nourishment—in orcas around the San Juans.

Whales vs people?

Cetaceans are merely among the more conspicuous players in Earth's ecological crisis, and the situation is likely to get worse before it can improve again. A 1970s environmental slogan is still pertinent—"Whatever your problem, it's a population problem." In a world of increasing human populations and declining food supplies, can—indeed should—whales be exempt from harvesting? All of us must find our own answers to that question, but let us consider that humans can choose to limit their own numbers before they destroy other species presently sharing our planet.

Whale Watching

The west coast attracts whale watchers from around the world. (DAES)

When humpback whaling started in 1907 from Page's Lagoon near Nanaimo, local residents complained about the smell. Elsewhere there were other complaints. J. A. Cates, manager of the Terminal Steamship Company in Vancouver, objected to whaling in Howe Sound to his member of parliament in Ottawa. Tourists in Vancouver took trips on Cates' steamers specifically to see whales. Was this the first commercial whale watching in Canada, or indeed the world? While discussion of Cates' complaint made the rounds of the Department of Marine and Fisheries, the last Howe Sound whale was killed by January 1908. A thriving whale watching industry was nipped in the bud.

The best way to experience whales, of course, is to see live ones. You can see a few species in captivity, usually at closer range than in the wild. Confinement in a relatively small space cramps the whales' natural behaviour, however. You can observe passing whales from shore in many West Coast spots, though you cannot usually approach closely. Best of all, you can go out on the sea and see whales for yourself in their own habitat.

Victoria is a major whale watching centre. (Maloff)

Whales on display

The glass-sided "water cage" allowed us to study marine animals as far back as 1832; by 1851 marine life was on display in the London Zoo. In 1861 Barnum exhibited belugas in New York, and the New York Aquarium showed bottlenose dolphins in 1913.

Whale watchers in a Zodiac experience whales close to sea level. (DAES)

These two pioneers introduced twin types of aquaria—private and public—that have continued ever since.

Private aquaria are built and operated as commercial attractions; they have no obligation to undertake research or education, though sometimes they facilitate research. They certainly give the public an opportunity to see and gain information about living marine creatures. Nonprofit public institutions, by contrast, are created with a mandate to undertake research and educate the public, though unless they receive significant public funding, they face similar pressure to attract enough visitors to support the operation.

By the twentieth century, many major North American cities had large private or public aquaria. Along with a great variety of fish, some exhibited dolphins and other small whales.

The first aquarium to feature whales as a major attraction was Marineland in Florida, built as a studio for underwater movie sequences; by 1937 its dolphins had become a public attraction in their own right. Marineland of the Pacific and others followed, displaying smaller dolphins, porpoises and even pilot whales. As aquaria aimed for ever larger audiences, they trained dolphins to leap through hoops and retrieve objects, making them seem as much fun as—and no more intelligent than—aquatic dogs. The public generally accepted this without question; controversy did not erupt in the aquarium world until the capture and captivity of orcas.

To people untroubled by cetaceans in captivity (see Chapter 8), aquaria offer the advantages of closer proximity to and better viewing of whales, perhaps underwater in a way impossible in the wild. A disadvantage is that no aquarium can have a tank big enough to show the range of natural behaviour of these highly intelligent and social animals, so that captive whales generally seem bored compared with wild whales.

Vancouver Aquarium

The Vancouver Aquarium opened in 1956 in Stanley Park, with financial support from city, province and federal governments and assistance from the University of British Columbia. Since then major donations and other fundraising have supported its growth, and its operations are self-supporting. It has several pools for marine mammals and its tanks hold more than 2 million gallons (9 million litres) of water. Its live cetaceans normally include not only West Coast orcas and Pacific white-sided dolphins but Arctic belugas.

Moby Doll – Orca by accident

The Vancouver Aquarium planned to have smaller whales, but felt that it would never be possible to display live orcas. Accordingly, it planned a life-size sculpture to represent the orca.

The sculptor hired for the job wanted a specimen to work from. In 1964 the aquarium set up a harpoon gun on Saturna Island, the southernmost Gulf Island. First the federal fisheries department, then a fishing company, provided a supporting boat. Almost two months later a whale was harpooned, but although the harpoon was firmly fixed the orca seemed otherwise uninjured. With much difficulty and trepidation, the aquarium brought the animal alive to temporary housing in an old Vancouver dock. Somewhat inadvertently, the aquarium had its—indeed, North America's—first captive orca.

Scientists flew in from across the continent, CBC played sound recordings nationwide, and other aquaria started to offer big dollars. The aquarium held a competition to name the orca, and from hundreds of entries chose the name Moby Doll. (Only on its death three months later did staff learn it was a male.) Aquarium director Murray Newman was named Vancouver's Man of the Year. Clearly the aquarium would display more orcas as soon as it could construct an adequate pool.

In 1966 the Vancouver Aquarium acquired three Pacific white-sided dolphins, which briefly occupied the new 125,000-gallon (570,000 L) pool but moved when a new orca arrived. A name-the-whale competition drew almost 6,000 submissions; Skana lived in captivity for more than thirteen years. Belugas first joined the collection in 1967 when specimens arrived from King Salmon, Alaska. They have done well in the aquarium and have usually been on display since. Less successful was an attempt to bring in narwhals from Pond Inlet on Baffin Island. After a 1968 exploratory trip, a 1970 trip brought back six young animals. They proved difficult to keep, and the last died within months.

Orcas have been a prime attraction at the Vancouver Aquarium, providing access to whales for many urban residents who cannot afford to go whale watching in the wild. (DAES)

In 1968 fishermen caught more orcas at Pender Harbour north of Vancouver. They sold some around the world, but the Vancouver Aquarium bought two which stayed at Pender for a while, attracting up to 1,200 visitors a day. In 1986 the aquarium opened its Max Bell Marine Mammal Centre, which included a 880,000-gallon (4 million L) killer whale habitat and a 440,000-gallon (2 million L) beluga habitat. Adjacent is the H. R. MacMillan gallery of whales, which gives an underwater view of the orcas and interprets whale biology with specimens, artifacts and sounds. Nearby are four labs, a library and a lecture theatre. (For information on the aquarium's scientific work, see Chapters 2 and 7.)

Vancouver Aquarium now attracts nearly a million people each year; its roughly 60,000 members include 200 volunteers. Aquarium insiders say that it has the world's finest orca exhibit and "most naturalistic interpretation of killer whale habitat and biology."

Other aquaria

In 1965 two fishermen in Namu, BC offered the Vancouver Aquarium two orcas that they had confined to a bay with nets. Every other aquarium in North America was also approached, however; to the fishermen the orcas represented dollars. One escaped and the other was purchased by Ted Griffin, the entrepreneur who had started the Seattle Aquarium. Namu lived for a year, launching Ted Griffin on a career as an orca hunter working in collaboration with other aquaria. In 1967 he captured an entire pod of orcas in Puget Sound. Two drowned in the nets, and other adults were released. But two were sold to San Diego aquaria and one to Vancouver, and Seattle Aquarium kept two.

Seattle was not content with orcas. In September 1979 a week-old female sperm whale stranded herself at Rockaway, Oregon. After a 300-mile (482 km) trip on a flatbed truck, this unlikely candidate for captivity arrived at Seattle Aquarium. The 12-foot (3.7 m), 800-pound (360 kg) baby was fed for a while on goat's milk, krill and vitamins, but soon died. The Seattle Aquarium no longer keeps cetaceans.

Another prominent commercial aquarium was Sealand in Oak Bay near Victoria. Restaurateur Bob Wright, impressed by the potential of the Vancouver Aquarium's 1968 Pender Harbour exhibit, opened it. Sealand of the Pacific was a floating whale pen in Oak Bay harbour. Its tank—separated from the sea by a net at one end and holding 1.5 million gallons (nearly 7 million L)—was then bigger than the Vancouver Aquarium's largest tank. Its first whale, the orca Haida, arrived in October 1968.

Haida comes when he's called, at Sealand in Oak Bay. This facility provided many opportunities for public viewing of whales until 1992 when it closed. (DAES)

Sealand offered a typical commercial exhibit, featuring Haida and albino orca Chimo in a circus-like display. Chimo, a female captured in Pedder Bay in 1970, lived for two and a half years. She attracted an offer of $1 million from a California aquarium, but Wright was not selling. Sealand, like the Vancouver Aquarium, suffered criticism for keeping orcas in captivity, which intensified in 1991 when the orcas drowned their young trainer Keltie Byrne.

Sealand closed the following year after the municipality refused to renew its licence.

Point Defiance Zoo and Aquarium at Tacoma, Washington, has displayed various cetaceans including harbor porpoises and belugas. The Oregon Coast Aquarium—opened in 1992 beside Newport's long established Hatfield Marine Science Center—has an annual attendance of around 600,000. Its original tanks held a million gallons (3.8 million L); a new 2 million-gallon (7.5 million L) open ocean pool opened in 1996 and housed the controversial orca Keiko for a while.

Bottlenose dolphins on the Prairies

The only inland—and indoor—live whale exhibit in western Canada is in the monster West Edmonton Mall in Edmonton, Alberta, promoted as the biggest shopping mall in the world. The dolphin pool is surrounded by 800 stores, a fun fair, ice rink, water park and a hotel. For ten years the pool has been home to several Atlantic bottlenose dolphins, which perform regularly for tired shoppers and fascinated tourists. Opponents of captive cetaceans are particularly uncomfortable with captivity in this context, though staff claim that the shows are educational and one dolphin—Maria—regularly does tricks for her own amusement before the mall opens.

Whale watching from land

"I was looking out of the window," said our dinner companion, "and saw this killer whale come right into the bay in front of us. A seal scrambled up onto the rocks, and the orca turned and went out again." Waterfront residents—even in urban Victoria—sometimes see a transient orca attempt to snatch a seal from under their noses. Although most land-based whale watching is not as exciting as this, it can often be rewarding. It is also less disturbing to whales than joining them in the water.

Signage gives information on the whales that pass San Juan Island's Lime Kiln Park along the "Orca freeway." (DAES)

Any frequenter of beaches and cliffs has occasional opportunities to see whales from land—it is a matter of being in the right place at the right time and keeping your eyes open. But you can enhance your chances by frequenting the same waters as the whales. Making local inquiries or reading local publications can often tell you which side of an island orcas usually use or when gray whales pass on migration. All coastal states and British Columbia offer opportunities to watch whales from land.

A few parks—near prime whale habitat—are known for the whale watching opportunities they offer. Lime Kiln State Whale Watch Park on the west coast of San Juan Island overlooks a prime orca highway. With binoculars you can pick out spouting gray whales in the Pacific almost any time they are migrating past Pacific Rim National Park on Vancouver Island. Seaside parks usually offer interpretation programs to help you understand the whales of the region. Between Christmas and New Year, volunteers at several sites in Oregon interpret the passing gray whales.

Park programs I sampled included an evening talk in the San Juans and a whale walk at Wickaninnish in Pacific Rim National Park.

Ed Spurr: whale talk at sunset

Ed Spurr was giving an evening talk in San Juan Island's San Juan County Park. I sat on the grass and listened as the sun gradually set and gilded the mackerel clouds. Ed was the grandson of a geologist and the son of a naturalist and had been involved with whales for a long time.

He told the group about the orcas of the region, how they differed from and resembled humans, and the impact of captures on the wild population. I learned that local people participated in the filming of *Free Willy 2* ("sixty islanders were extras") and of an attempt to educate amateur whale watchers in responsible behaviour. ("If we see a boat getting too close we give them literature and explain.")

Most interesting to us was the question period, which revealed other visitors' knowledge and background about whales, and some of Ed's views on the questions of the day. How did he feel about captive whales? someone asked. "They did a pretty good job of letting us get to know them, but perhaps we should let them go now."

One of the audience was concerned about the carnivorous diet of transient whales—couldn't we give them something else to eat? Ed said, straight-faced, "There doesn't seem to be any shortage of humans."

Our whale walk started from the Wickaninnish Centre, which combines an elegant restaurant with a whale exhibit. We headed along the shore as park naturalist David Pitt-Brooke explained the biology of the gray whale. From the pockets of his gear David produced a sperm whale tooth and a piece of baleen. The beach provided sand hoppers (related to krill) at the appropriate place in his story.

Trained as a vet in Saskatoon, later a park naturalist in the mountains, David enjoyed being back at the coast—he had lived in Prince Rupert as a child. Between stops we enjoyed the surf on the rocks, watched the gulls and eagles and talked to other visitors in the party. Tourists from Japan had been given unrealistic expectations and wanted to know if we were going to feed the whales. "No," explained David patiently, "but we should see some." On the rocks at the end of the walk we patiently watched the gray sea but saw no spouts. Sometimes the whales just don't read the books.

David and Pam Nyman, whale watchers

It's a long way from York, England, to the small village of Tofino on Vancouver Island's west coast, but David and Pam Nyman had read about gray whales and decided that they really wanted to see them in the wild. There was only one problem—both Nymans suffered from seasickness.

At first they tried hiking the Whale Watching Trail to prominent bluffs in Pacific Rim Park, but low cloud and intermittent showers meant that they couldn't see anything even if the whales were out there. They screwed up their courage and boarded a whale watching boat. They bobbed around miserably for what seemed like hours (but was probably only ninety minutes), when suddenly a large back broke the water ahead. Instantly their seasickness vanished. Their next sighting was the whale's flukes. "Now that was worth it," Pam remarked quietly.

The Nymans were on the West Coast for three weeks and saw the whales for only a few moments, but it didn't matter. "It is so wonderful to see whales in the wild instead of an aquarium. Some day we'll be back to do it again." —AJS

A killer whale blows. (Morton R)

Whale watching on the water

Anywhere you travel on the sea you may see whales. Ferries in Alaska, British Columbia and Washington state provide many opportunities to see orcas, dolphins and sometimes other species, and captains often mention sightings over the intercom. Ferries have schedules to keep, however, and unless the courses of whale and ferry are parallel, you are unlikely to see them very closely. At the other extreme, you may go in your own boat—owned, borrowed or rented—to watch whales to your heart's content, subject only to rules prohibiting their harassment.

Several whale watching centres provide opportunities to sail to the whales. (DAES)

Most people experience meaningful whale watching on the water courtesy of a whale watching business that takes out groups for anything from a few hours to a week or two. Modern whale watching reputedly started in California in 1955 with a single boat out of San Diego, taking visitors to the gray whale's breeding lagoons. A recently published guide to West Coast whale watching lists almost 150 businesses operating cruises between Alaska and California. With such variety, how can you choose where to go and in what kind of craft?

Where to go

Where you go depends on what you want to see, how much time and money you can spare and how you would like to travel.

The main choices are:

• a part-day or day trip by small boat from a small port near where whales appear regularly

• a two-day to two-week cruise on a larger boat or ship out of a major port (San Diego, Seattle, Vancouver)

Costs for cruises range from hundreds to thousands of dollars, so they may seem expensive compared to a part- or full-day trip for under $100. Remember, however, that the farther you travel from your home—or, if you come from outside the region, from major airports such as Seattle and Vancouver—the more expensive the trip. Also, day trips do not include local travel, accommodation or meals.

Most short whale watching trips focus on places where one or more species can be seen reliably; on a longer cruise you can expect to see whales at one or more points. Alaska, British Columbia and Washington state all offer both outer waters and sheltered inner waters, while Oregon has only an outer coast. California offers trips to offshore islands and, on longer trips, access to the Mexican breeding grounds of the gray whale.

• Alaska offers—depending on location—humpback whales, grays, and harbor and Dall's porpoises, with the possibility of seeing fins and Minkes, seis, orcas and Pacific white-sided dolphins.

A group of whale watchers look out eagerly. Who'll spot the first blow? (Dennis)

- British Columbia offers grays and orcas, with the possibility of seeing blue, fin, humpbacks, Minkes, Pacific white-sided dolphins and even sperm whales.
- Washington state offers grays, Minkes, orcas and the possibility of seeing harbor porpoises and Pacific white-sided dolphins.
- Oregon offers grays and a chance of seeing Dall's and harbor porpoises, humpbacks and orcas.
- California offers grays, orcas and a chance of seeing blues and humpbacks.

To choose a location, ask the province or state tourism department for free information or consult a recent whale watching guide. (See Resources for phone numbers and suggested publications.) Even if your dedication to whales is monomaniacal, you will pursue other activities on your visit, so consider a base that would be fun even if you don't go out to sea—after all, you may be waiting for the whales.

Orcas sometimes "porpoise" along the surface like smaller whales. (Baird)

When to go

No matter how careful your planning, bear in mind that whales are not entirely predictable. I did a research trip to the San Juans at prime whale watching time, but the whales had headed up Vancouver Island's west coast—perhaps on their holidays? I interviewed people I wanted to meet, but there were no orcas to be seen.

When you choose holiday dates for the best watching experience, consider the movements of migrating whales, the likely weather and the activities of your fellow humans. The gray whale migration is one of the most predictable, and it is easy to work out where and when to see the main passage north and south. Remember, some whales drop out of the migration to hang around off the coast after the main party heads north. (For whale migration schedules, see Resources.) Orcas normally swim in Washington's Puget Sound and British Columbia's Strait of Georgia waters through the summer; humpbacks appear in most summer—and some winter—months in Alaska.

What to take

On a sunny day, you can enjoy whale watching in a T-shirt, shorts and sneakers—but whatever the weather when you set out, expect conditions to change. It's a good idea to take:

- Windproof, waterproof outer clothing (unless your whale watching outfit supplies survival suits)
- More warm clothes than you think you will need, including long pants and sweater
- A hat that will not blow off
- Sunscreen

Also useful can be:

- Binoculars (one pair per person if possible)
- Field guides to marine mammals and sea birds
- Camera
- Short telephoto lens
- More film than you think you will need
- Videorecorder
- Notebook
- Chart or map of the region
- Things to amuse the kids when you are not seeing whales
- Small packsack to put all this stuff in
- A drink, sandwich or health bar per person (if no food is provided)

Looking for humpbacks off Kodiak Island in November—the time of greatest abundance—you would certainly dress for cold. California might be too hot for comfort in the same month. The Pacific Northwest generally has fine long summer days (though heavy morning fog may linger by the sea). Early spring and late fall days, however, can be gloomy and wet, so that even if whales are around you may not see them well. Trips on the sea are at the mercy of rough weather, particularly on the outer coast where even in calm weather there is likely to be a heavy swell. Storms can come at any time, but are more likely in spring and fall than in summer.

Summer brings better transportation and accommodation, but also more people competing for services. Other pertinent human activities include special whale watching weeks (Oregon, spring and fall) and festivals, such as Tofino and Ucluelet's Whale Festival in March and April and the Festival of Whales on the San Juans in May. Advantages include lectures and other special programs to enhance your enjoyment; disadvantages include more of your fellow humans than you might wish. Conditions may be less crowded if you can time your trips for midweek. Remember that in the fall peak salmon season, many whale watching boats miraculously become fishing charter boats.

Choosing your boat

A part-day trip is most people's first whale watching experience. Choose your boat to suit your answers to diverse questions. How small a boat do you feel comfortable in? Have you ever paddled a kayak? Do you have the leisure for a sailboat trip? How important is it to see whales on this trip? What do you already know about whales? How often do you use the washroom?

Do you get seasick?

Are you likely to be seasick? Do you know? In quiet inland waters you normally don't have to worry, but the misnamed Pacific always has a swell, and rough weather is possible anywhere. Poor sailors, even experienced ones encountering different waters, may find it worth choosing a larger boat and taking precautions.

Various antidotes for seasickness are available. Drug stores sell nonprescription tablets to take before your trip—if you are already feeling ill, it is too late. Ask about side effects, which may include drowsiness. You can also buy (or some outfits supply) a wristband that presses on an acupressure point. Various folk remedies may or may not work; one of our captains swore by a bit of fresh ginger held between teeth and gums. If you know you have a problem, talk to your doctor, who may prescribe a scopolamine patch worn behind your ear.

At the busiest places, your choices may be between small, medium and large power boats, sailboats and kayaks. For the beginner, the best choice is a medium-sized power boat, covered against the weather but allowing access to the outer decks, big enough to have a head (washroom), an upper deck for a more distant view and—particularly on the outer coasts—stability in a swell.

The crew is as important as the boat. Does your skipper spend most of his or her time leading whale tours, or does the outfit just turn up briefly in peak periods to skim the cream? Is your skipper a responsible mariner, or a cowboy who thinks slamming onto every wave is the best part of the ride? Can she find whales, behave ethically around them and knowledgeably explain what you see? Does he support or participate in local whale research? The skipper is the key person, possibly supported by an experienced naturalist. Some boats have hydrophones which allow you to hear whales underwater.

Loading kayaks at the dock in Telegraph Cove, a prime centre for many tours that provide opportunities to paddle with the whales. (DAES)

Earl Thomas, whaleboat skipper

"I'm in heaven," said Earl Thomas, the First Nations whaleboat skipper for Chinook Charters who took us out from Tofino. "It's hard to categorize this as work. There's no two days alike. There's nothing I'd rather do."

Raised in Port Alberni, Earl lives in Ucluelet and seems right at home at the helm of his boat, where he spends nine months of the year. Outside whale season it's a water taxi, with a covered cabin, head and open rear deck. This day it carried an enthusiastic group of would-be whale watchers. First we went to see a bald eagle's nest with the female sitting. "She's been on the eggs a few days," explained the captain. Then we turned out of the harbour into choppy water in the roughest part of the trip. Once we were beyond the breakers we turned south, hoping to meet gray whales heading north. "There's one," he pointed out, "near that island covered with dog hair." And indeed, in front of the distant tree-covered island, a whale spouted. We turned, waited for it to come up and followed at a distance along the shore. "You get males at this time," we were told. "The females and calves come at the end of April, and they're real skittish. In summer, the resident whales are more tolerant of boats, but they're basically feeding." Gently we drifted north with the whales, occasional spouting on all sides. Earl quietly filled us in on gray whale biology and told stories of the sometimes unrealistic expectations of visitors and—when we asked—his more remarkable experiences. "Some people are really disappointed, they expect them to jump through hoops," he said, "but sometimes they're lucky. The 'friendlies' will come right up to the boat, and people can scratch them." Most exciting were encounters with transient killer whales. "One group spotted a gray whale spout and chased the female right up to the side of the boat. She had her fin up and her head. She rolled upside down lifting the baby on her belly. There were five killer whales behind her, and they let her go. Another time I had a Steller's sea lion trying to jump in the boat to escape from three orcas."

A smaller cabin cruiser may take only a small group, giving more flexibility, but your skipper may know more about fishing than about whales. A Zodiac—a small, fast, inflatable power boat—can provide a thrilling ride, especially in rough water, but will lack shelter and washrooms.

A sailboat provides a more leisurely, quiet trip, which can be a delight in itself even if you do not see whales. A sailboat does not have the flexibility to follow quickly after a new sighting, however, and if it does so under power you might as well be in a power boat.

An experienced kayaker can feel more closely attuned to the water and psychologically closer to whales than any other traveller, but a novice may be wiser to get the hang of a kayak without distractions. Novice or not, you can't easily follow a pod of whales that passes by, though on a multi-day trip in whale waters you have a good chance of a close encounter. If whales come to you, they can seem awfully big. As Alexandra Morton points out, "you wouldn't want to get that close to a bear."

The **Lady Selkirk** *is one of the larger whale watching boats to sail out of Tofino. (DAES)*

Some kayakers are lucky enough to have a close--and perhaps even a little scary--encounter. (Maloff)

Disabled adults using wheelchairs can often be accommodated on larger boats, but may have trouble getting to washrooms down ladders or through narrow doors. Be sure to ask. Children can function well on any kind of boat, but may prefer larger vessels which give them more room to move around. If you cannot guarantee good behaviour, take your family in a small cabin cruiser with no other passengers.

When you book, ask what is included. Some outfits provide cruiser suits or other protective clothing; some supply meals, depending on the length of the trip. You don't normally have to book before you arrive unless you pay a short visit at a peak period, though it would help to phone ahead to the local chamber of commerce or one or two whale watching outfits before deciding your destination. It is often possible to arrive, go for a successful whale watching trip and be on your way later the same day. In peak periods, though, busy places book ahead or turn people away.

If you spend two or three days at the base port, you improve your chances of a good time. You can enjoy the community (which often has other attractions), find out where to park before you sail, look at boats arriving and departing, talk to other travellers, check the weather forecast and compare prices. Your key question is, how active are the whales? The *Island Independent* in the San

Juans summarizes whale hotline information, or you can ask around. With this information, you can book the trip you expect to enjoy most. Depending on your success, you can then head for home or try another trip with the same captain or another charter. Every trip is different, and there is no certainty of success.

Outfits that offer "guaranteed whale sightings" are only offering a free trip next day if you see nothing—and may count a distant dolphin as a sighting. Ask what the guarantee means.

Photographing whales

"To anyone who is in search of real excitement I can heartily recommend camera hunting for whales," said Roy Chapman Andrews in 1916. Since then cameras have improved, films are faster, and if you miss your first shot, whalers don't harpoon your subject before you can try again—but otherwise it's still true.

Three key things are worth remembering about whale photography. First, prepare properly. If you are unfamiliar with your camera, work out the bugs before your trip. And you never have enough film. Take a range of film—high speeds will improve your chances of getting clear pictures, but you may need a slower film if the day is bright. A small telephoto lens can be useful, but unless you are in quiet inland waters in a large boat, you probably can't stand still long enough to use a large one.

Experienced photographers wait for the best shot. (DAES)

Second, remember to take pictures—many people find the sight of living whales so enthralling that they stand open-mouthed and forget to lift the camera. Don't rest your camera on the rail or another solid part of the boat, or vibration may spoil your pictures. Be ready for brief appearances. You can roughly predict the emergence of whales swimming in a regular pattern, but you will still end up with a lot of shots of water where they have just been. The more extreme behaviour—spyhops, breaches—can be much harder to predict. One second you are looking at a blank open sea and the next second there is a whale in midair—you must be ready and snap fast. Under these conditions, focussing can be a problem—if you don't have autofocus, use a floating log or another whale watching boat to get an idea of distance before you try the whales. If you are lucky, the whale may repeat its behaviour, but if possible catch it the first time.

The third thing? Oh yes—stop taking photos from time to time and just enjoy what you see. You'll miss the essence of the experience if you have to wait for your developed photos to see what you saw.

On the day of your trip, get there in good time to find parking (which may be some distance away), queue for the washroom and perhaps choose and struggle into a cruiser suit. Your captain will brief you about safety procedures and let you know what has been seen lately. Prepare to enjoy the whole trip and look for seals and birds as well as whales. On board, walk the ship—if it's big enough—to locate good observation positions and the head. Get to know your fellow passengers—they are likely to be interesting people—and follow your route on your map if you have one. Enjoy the other wildlife as you see it—when you make contact with whales, you will have eyes for little else.

Out with the orcas

"Nobody's going to come up here to look at blackfish," old-timer Fred Wastell told Bill MacKay when he proposed whale watching from Telegraph Cove on Vancouver Island. But since 1980 Bill, his wife Donna and current proprietor Jim Borrowman have had a thriving business—Stubbs Island Charters—which now uses two boats and takes out 200 visitors a day in peak season.

I went out with Jim one September afternoon in the *Lukwa*, their new purpose-built whale watching boat. The morning trip had been out in mist—they saw lots of Pacific white-sided dolphins but no orcas, and as Jim had warned us, "you can't pull whales out of a hat." But the weather was sunny and we were prepared to enjoy ourselves. We watched Telegraph Cove fall behind us and looked around at the opening vista of glassy sea, islands and distant mountains.

"Leave me alone for twenty minutes while I check in with the researchers around," said Jim, "and then you can take turns to join me on the bridge." On the radio, he talked to the network of researchers working nearby and anyone else passing through. Someone in a plane reported an orca sighting, and we headed off to check it out.

We passed a young eagle on the nest and a couple of seals on a rock close to submergence with the rising tide, but the seals were resting and Jim didn't go too close. Suddenly dolphins appeared, and Jim switched off the motor. For half an hour we sat quietly in the water with the dolphins playing all around us, weaving in and out and jumping joyfully into the air. Jim threw the hydrophone overboard, and we could hear their calls while we watched. It is hard to be objective and scientific about them—they are so obviously having a good time, and I recalled my conversation a few days earlier with ferry steward Mary Abbot. "It would be good to be reincarnated as a killer whale," she had said quietly, "people have a lot of respect for them. But then I look at the dolphins—they have a lot of fun."

The Gikumi *is one of two large boats that sail out of Telegraph Cove in search of orcas. (DAES)*

As the dolphins wandered off, we started again and headed in a different direction, following a different plane's lead on other orcas. We headed across a strait past rafts of sooty shearwaters and a lot of drifting logs. In the distance, Jim confidently identified a bobbing lump as an elephant seal. As we approached an island a couple of hours into our trip, all binoculars were trained ahead. Sure enough, a blow and a black fin told us that we had connected. As we approached a group of slowly moving orcas, Stubbs' other boat, the *Gikumi*, and a Zodiac from another outfit joined us; it buzzed noisily into the place the pod had been as we approached. As we got closer, the unflappable Jim got excited. He can identify at a glance most orcas in the region, but these he didn't know. Photos were desirable, but he had left his cameras on the other boat. With care, the two vessels approached, and an aluminum box was handed across carefully. Then the boats moved slowly in parallel to the pod, cameras clicking whenever they surfaced in unison. The whales seemed to sense our excitement and some of them started breaching—once or twice each. A rainbow-coloured float plane passed overhead. With great care it landed at a distance ahead of the orcas, cut the engines and waited for the procession to come by. For perhaps an hour we parallelled the orcas, and Jim tentatively recognized a mix of two infrequently seen pods. Then we headed for home, happily punch-drunk with sunshine, sightings and adrenalin, no longer the same people we had been when we went out.

The following day I watched the morning sailing set out, wondering if they would be as unsuccessful as the last morning sailing. As they headed out of the cove I heard a shout—the orcas were right there waiting for them, so close that I could see them from the dock.

On your own

If you have access to a boat, you can watch whales on your own timetable and spend as much time as you wish with them. Laws in both the USA and Canada protect whales from harassment, and guidelines can show how you should behave to avoid causing them problems. It is important to know and follow these guidelines. You can't approach whales too closely, but they may decide to approach you! But you are on your own in more than one sense. You have to do your own identifications. Furthermore, the information you gather may be helpful to researchers, and it becomes your responsibility to pass it on.

What did you see?

On a formal whale watching trip, the skipper or naturalist will usually do the identification for you.

On your own, it's not always so easy. For your own satisfaction, you need to observe and record data to make a proper identification, which is particularly important if you are recording the sighting to help local researchers. Use a camera if possible, and also record in a notebook any visible features of the whale.

Appearance:

- Colour and pattern
- Dorsal fin or hump
- Flukes if seen
- Size (in comparison with anything measurable, such as the size of your boat)

Behaviour:

- Manner in which whale surfaces and dives
- Blow—single or double, direction
- Number in pod
- Activity (swimming, loafing, spyhopping, breaching, etc.)
- Direction in which whales are heading

Situation:

- Date, time
- Location as accurately as possible
- Weather
- Sea conditions
- Light direction (can cause you to miss white patches if the whale is silhouetted)

Observer(s):

- Name of vessel
- Observer(s), contact address or phone
- Experience of observers in region and with species

Even pilots of passing planes are not immune to the fascination of whales, and sometimes drop in to take a close look. (DAES)

Safety afloat

No guidelines prevent whales from harassing you; fortunately they would rarely be necessary. Jim Darling tells of a gray whale that rammed a policeman's boat off Long Beach. The policeman came to Darling, worried about a possible threat to other boaters. Darling asked if it had rolled belly-up, and when the policeman nodded, explained that it was a "friendly" that just wanted to be patted.

On the other hand, accidents do occur. Recently a humpback breached onto the bow of a boat in Alaska. In another incident, a bowhead overturned a boat, drowning four people. And while there are no fully documented records of deliberate orca attacks on humans, if you are in or close to the water, it would be wise to treat transients with respect.

Even without inadvertent aggression by whales, some risk accompanies any voyage. Tragedies are infrequent in proportion to the many whale watchers, but two March 1998 fatalities in rough water off Tofino remind us that they can happen.

Icy swim

When Nicky Graham went whale watching in Alaska in July 1995, she anticipated some excitement, but she didn't expect a swim with a whale. Nicky knows her whales—with her husband Pip she had been volunteering for seven years to assist whale researchers in Hawaii and Alaska. The small party was a couple of hours out from Petersburg in a 28-foot aluminum boat, skippered by Steve Berry, when they met about twenty humpbacks feeding near the Fingers Islands.

The whales were quietly feeding, though a couple breached in the distance. Two moved closer to the boat, which was idling quietly in the water. "I was standing on the starboard side holding a hydrophone," remembers Nicky, "when the captain said 'I think that whale is going to breach.' As he said it, it came up right beside the boat, twisting as it came. Its head hit the bow, and its pec fin swept the starboard side, and took the railings off the boat, along with me and two others.

"I remember being in the water, with the white bottom of the boat above me, and the fin below me. We came right back with the splash that fills the vacuum behind the whale, and all three of us were rescued."

The boat suffered $31,000 in damages, but despite some bruising and five minutes in the water at 44 degrees, Nicky and her fellow travellers—all good swimmers—came to no harm. In our conversation, Nicky's main anxiety was that I might think the whale deliberately attacked the boat. "There was no aggression at all as far as the whale was concerned," she said. "It was unfortunate timing. But I wasn't scared at all—I know whales." After a brief stay in hospital, Nicky was back whale watching.

Orconomics

How can we measure the importance of whale watching? On land we have killed off most animals bigger than ourselves, but in the sea it is still possible to meet such creatures. But how can we calculate the value of beauty or the importance of an awe-inspiring encounter with the wild? How can we use such ephemeral experiences to convince our decision makers of the importance of protecting the wild before it is too late?

These are intangibles. But orca economist Erich Hoyt has been busy with his calculator, producing statistics to impress any business person or politician.

In our region whale watching brings in an estimated annual $4.5 to $6 million in Oregon, Washington, British Columbia and Alaska, with whale-related items valued at about half as much again. How much would these amounts increase if we could reliably find gray whales and Minkes in the Strait of Juan de Fuca or humpbacks in Saanich Inlet and Howe Sound? A bigger picture is even more impressive. In 1992 worldwide whale watching attracted almost four and a half million people, who spent $75 million on tickets and $318 million in total revenues. Over 75 percent of those whale watchers were North Americans.

No one seems to have totalled whale research, conservation and interpretation budgets for the same region, but—with few paid researchers and uncertain field funds—no doubt they are minuscule by comparison. Tofino whale watching outfits collect a dollar a head from whale watchers to fund research programs; we would do well to follow suit elsewhere. Whaling showed the vulnerability of whale stocks to unscientifically based hunting. Whales are now more valuable alive than dead; let us not grudge funds for ongoing research and conservation that help keep them that way.

Jamie's whaling station in Tofino invites you to follow the flukes. (DAES)

Whale Cultures

This Makah hunter was photographed early in this century, in traditional style with harpoon and sealskin floats. (VMM)

When the Vancouver Aquarium chose an orca as the subject of an entrance sculpture, it chose as sculptor a leading figure in the revival of First Nations art. Bill Reid's *The Chief of the Undersea World* appropriately celebrates the important place of whales in West Coast culture since the earliest times. The spectacular bronze has been on display since 1984.

Chief of the Undersea World

Bill Reid's Chief of the Undersea World *dominates the entrance to the Vancouver Aquarium. (DAES)*

After donors offered to fund the project, the aquarium reviewed several artists' work before selecting Bill Reid (1920–98), who shared the Haida heritage through his mother. Not content merely to copy traditional styles in traditional materials, he expanded the concept of Native art into larger scale works and borrowed materials from other artistic traditions. Thus he executed his splendid 18-foot (5.5 m) orca sculpture in bronze.

In his sixties and suffering from Parkinson's disease, Reid first considered granite as a medium but felt that he could no longer handle the physical work involved. Eventually, recalling that the Haida viewed copper as a noble metal, he suggested bronze. He carried out the demanding commission with the help of other artists and a New York foundry. Beginning with a small boxwood model based on a Haida speaker's staff in the Smithsonian, Reid and his helpers spent six months creating first a 4-foot (1.2 m) maquette and then a full-size plaster model of the sculpture, detailing its surface in traditional style. The assembled model would barely squeeze into Reid's crowded Granville Island studio. Trucked to New York in sections, the model was cast in ten pieces of bronze, welded together, acid treated and waxed to produce the patina. Erected over a 20-foot (6 m) reflecting pool, *The Chief of the Undersea World* can be admired by one and all as a splendid work of art. It also reminds us of the importance of the orca in First Nations tradition and the aquarium's important role in bringing the impressive toothed whales to the attention of millions of visitors.

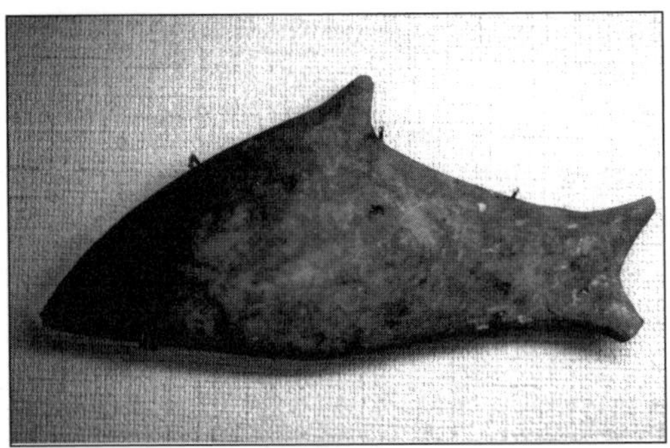

This orca stone carving is from the excavation of a 2,000-year-old site on Pender Island. (DAES)

Whales have always been part of West Coast culture. For coastal First Nations, whales were more than a source of food and materials—they permeated the entire social and imaginative life of the people. They have similarly affected later residents, particularly ethnic groups such as the Japanese, who also have a long cultural connection with whales. Whatever their origins, all who have lived on and by the sea have developed an intellectual and emotional relationship with cetaceans.

Our modern society has gone beyond exploitation to create a whale culture based on scientific research, interpretation and popular enjoyment of whales in our arts and other cultural dimensions. We can be deeply involved with West Coast whales without ever seeing a live cetacean. This chapter shows some ways in which whales indirectly influence our culture.

Pretending to be a whale

Petroglyphs of unknown antiquity—found on the coast from Washington state to Alaska—show that First Peoples have long known that whales were more than useful resources in large packages. Indeed, human interactions with whales have been far richer and more complex than they first appear. First Nations slaughtered whales for food and other resources, but they greatly respected

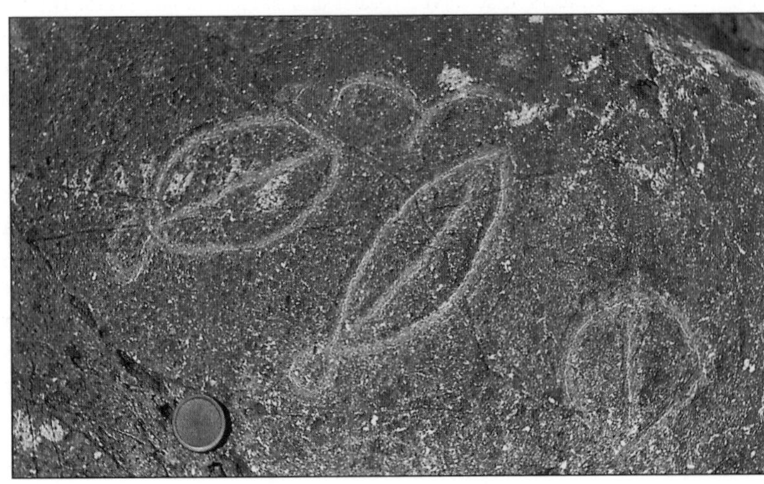

These whale petroglyphs on the Olympic Peninsula are of unknown age, but hint at the antiquity of First Nations' interest in whales. (DAES)

their prey. The whale hunt was only one important part whales played in their culture.

Among the Nuu-chah-nulth, whale hunting was controlled by a chief who had the spiritual power to bring drifting whales to the shore and the skill to hunt them. A Makah helper at the Ozette excavation remembered similar traditions. "My dad used to pray and prepare himself for months...He knew special songs to bring power and had magic amulets and charms he kept in a secret place and wouldn't let the rest of us see. Sometimes he would swim out around the rocks beyond the surf, diving and spouting like a whale. He was pretending to be a whale to show that his heart was right. A man needed all the spirit power he could get when he led his crew on a hunt." The chief's wife had to remain passive, tended by others, until the whale was caught. First Nations whalers in the 1990s are continuing the same traditions.

Although whaling was clearly important to the Nuu-chah-nulth, one observer said it "captured the imaginations of both the Nutkans and the anthropologists who have written about them," and that perhaps its cultural importance has been exaggerated. This is not an uncommon phenomenon. A picturesque phrase expresses a similar thought about inland cultures, where people have been said to "talk moose, eat rabbit."

The whalers' shrine

In the early nineteenth century whalers built a shrine at a secret location on an island in Jewett's Lake, near Friendly Cove on Vancouver Island. They built a house which eventually filled with eighty-eight carved images of dead whalers, four carved whales and sixteen human skulls. The Nuu-chah-nulth considered these significant in rituals designed to attract whales to come to shore and beach themselves. In the shrine, Yuquot chiefs purified themselves with water and hemlock boughs and slept on a pallet of human skulls.

During the search for anthropological materials, in 1904 George Hunt bought the entire shrine for the American Museum of Natural History in New York, which regarded it as his most important acquisition. Hunt was part Scots and part Tlingit and was raised speaking Kwakwala. The Nuu-chah-nulth first required him to prove that he was himself a shaman; then local chiefs took him to visit the shrine in 1903 or 1904.

Hunt eventually bought the shrine for $500 and ten sacred songs from two Kwakwa'ka'wakw chiefs, valuable properties available only by purchase or gift. He had to wait until people were away sealing and canning before he could remove it.

Despite its importance, the American Museum has never displayed the shrine. The Nuu-chah-nulth were moved inland to Gold River, where pulp mill pollution and cultural conflict have presented problems. Anthropologists Aldona Jonaitis of the American Museum and Richard Inglis of the Royal British Columbia Museum are now collaborating on a book about the shrine. In 1989 they went to Gold River to meet the elders, and Chief Jerry Jack expressed his appreciation that, for the first time, the museums had come to discuss the shrine. In 1990 the chiefs were invited to New York and now wish to create a new shrine as the centrepiece of a planned cultural centre.

Porpoise potlatch and whale milk

People have never stopped telling stories about whales. First Nations and fishermen, whalers and whale watchers—all delight in stories fantastic and factual. A Quileute story explains how Whale gave a potlatch for his daughter, Miss Porpoise, which broke up in a fight. Cougar scratched Whale, making the grooves on his underside and causing him and his daughter to take refuge in the sea.

The West Coast character By-God Stafford told a tall tale of a whale in the bay who had lost her calf and came every morning to be milked. "I filled the canoe right full and I had to go ashore and get the 18-foot rowboat, by-god. They give a lot of milk, those whales..."

Some whalers became legendary characters whose exploits are still told on bridges and in bars. One was the gloomy Norwegian gunner Moses Erikson, who got depressed and drank the alcohol from his compass. Another was Knut Halvorsen, who pursued an injured whale in the darkness with a flashlight and brought it in. Captain Heater rigged lines to a whale and steered his ship with it when it broke his rudder, while in 1916 the *Orion* was damaged by an unexploded bomb which went off when the whale was towed beside the ship.

There are many tales of a carelessly secured harpoon gun that swung around and went off pointing backward, firing an explosive harpoon through the bridge. Others tell of whale flensers at a dance who—no matter how many times they had washed—were identified by the smell of whale by the local girls after one circuit of the dance floor. Salt Spring Islanders still tell of the stranded whale that decayed until it exploded—blubber hung up in the trees for weeks—while an Internet favourite is Dave Barry's story of a whale exploded to remove it from an Oregon beach.

The oral story tradition lives on among modern British Columbia storytellers. Robert Minden has recorded his story *The Boy Who Wanted to Talk to Whales*, complete with wonderful music played on a variety of found objects.

Whale Lit 101

If Herman Melville had not jumped ship from the *Acushnet* in the Marquesas in 1842, he would have ended up on the West Coast. Then perhaps our region would have featured in *Moby Dick*, the world's most famous whaling novel. Melville did not regard right whale hunting as sporting, however: "The Right Whale on the Nor'West Coast, in chill and dismal fogs, the sullen inert monsters...submitting to the harpoon like half stunned bullocks to the knife; this horrid and indecent Right whaling..." Melville didn't visit British Columbia, but Mount Moby Dick and several other peaks in British Columbia's Selkirk Mountains bear names from his works. For those who ponder such hypothetical questions as why there isn't a Canadian *Moby Dick*, novelist and poet Margaret Atwood has the answer. "If a Canadian did a *Moby Dick*, it would be done from the point of view of the whale."

A few of the many books that make up a west coast whale library. (DAES)

Whales play a part in British Columbia literature. Poets inspired by whales include bill bissett and Susan Musgrave. Vancouver writer Lloyd Abbey has celebrated the blue in *The Last Whale*, while both Audrey Thomas's story "Aquarius" and Laurence Gough's detective story *Killers*—in which a human body is found floating in the killer whale pool—are set at the Vancouver Aquarium. In the USA, marine mammal biologist Victor Scheffer has used his expert knowledge to fictionalize the life of a sperm whale in his novel *The Year of the Whale.*

Both countries produce many stories for children featuring whales. Fine titles include Roderick Haig-Brown's evocation of Nuu-chah-nulth culture in *The Whale People*, Alexandra Morton's *Siwiti* and Paul Lewis's beautifully illustrated *Storm Boy.*

The richest cetacean literature in the region is perhaps nonfiction;

more recent work often reflects "the point of view of the whale." Classics such as Scammon's *Marine Mammals* (1874, 1968) and the almost unobtainable *Whale Hunting with Gun and Camera* (Andrews, 1916, 1931) give a broad contemporary view of whales and whaling. Hagelund's *Whalers No More* gives a vivid first-hand account of the whaler's life, while Webb's *On the Northwest* and Goddard's *Window on Whaling* provide valuable histories of whaling.

More modern books about whales themselves include editor Haley's *Marine Mammals of Eastern North Pacific and Arctic Waters*, Obee and Ellis' *Guardians of the Whales* and D'Vincent's *Voyaging with the Whales.* Individual species have been studied by Busch in *Gray Whales,* Hand in *Gone Whaling* and Hoyt in *Orca—the Whale Called Killer.* Conservation history is presented in Hunter's *Warriors of the Rainbow* and Weyler's *Song of the Whale.*

We are fortunate to have autobiographies by Andrews and Scheffer, and by Murray Newman of the Vancouver Aquarium, but do not yet have adult biographical books on or by other major researchers. Perhaps the best pictures of a whale researcher at work come from Alexandra Morton's books for children.

Alexandra Morton, researcher and writer

As a child in the mountains of Connecticut, Alexandra Morton knew little about the sea and even less about whales. "I was a total misfit in school," she told us. "I had no interest in sports or boys or dolls—I liked the frog pond." At age ten she heard of Jane Goodall's research with chimpanzees and found a role model for women in science—"Jane Goodall has been my idol all my life." Later, in Los Angeles, she worked with dolphin psychologist John Lilly, studying captive orcas from the Pacific Northwest. When their calves died, however, Alex decided to investigate their wild relatives.

Alexandra Morton. (DAES)

In her early twenties in 1978, when she started work on the underwater sounds of orcas, "it felt like the beginning of my life." In 1980 she met Robin Morton filming the same pod of whales. They married and raised money by filming and chartering their boat until they could begin joint research on a year-round study of orca vocalizations. By the time they had raised enough funds in 1984, their son Jarret had arrived. Tragically, Robin died in a diving accident in 1986.

Courageously, Alexandra continued her work on orcas and more recently on Pacific white-sided dolphins and the wider marine ecology. At first she and Jarret lived on a floating house, then in the tiny community of Simoom Sound on an island three hours from Port McNeill. She supported herself by selling photographs and making T-shirts. "I like a business one could drop and run out of the door" whenever the whales came by. With a new partner—and a new child—Alex continues to work on the whales. She has written and illustrated two books about whales, *Siwiti—A Whale's Story* (1991) and *In the Company of Whales* (1993), both appropriately released by Orca Publishing in Victoria. (*Siwiti* won the Sheila A. Egoff Children's Book Prize.) Alexandra's books and articles give a fascinating picture of the life of an independent researcher and of the scientific and personal discoveries that it is possible to make a "living near whales and trying to fit in."

Whale music

Whales have been making sounds for millions of years, but humans recognized some of their noises as songs in 1970. Researcher Roger Payne issued a record, *Songs of the Humpback Whale*, which sold more than 100,000 copies. It was popular with counterculture people, some of whom listened to it after taking LSD to produce mystical experiences, but also fascinated a wider public.

Paul Winter plays his sax to the whales on the 1975 Greenpeace expedition. (Weyler)

More recently, direct broadcasts have become possible with ORCA FM (88.5), broadcasting live sound from Johnstone Strait orcas locally and (by land line) to the Vancouver Aquarium.

Human musicians have collaborated musically with whales, incorporating their fascinating sounds into various compositions. Most notable perhaps is "And God Created Great Whales," by the American composer Alan Hovhaness, recorded by the Seattle Symphony and performed by the Vancouver Symphony at the opening of the Vancouver Aquarium's Max Bell Marine Mammal Centre. Whalers have been singing about their work for several centuries, but surprisingly few songs relate to the north Pacific. "Off to Sea Once More," sometimes sung by the Bering Sea bowhead fishermen, gives a vivid picture of the whalers' life, while "Rolling Down to Old Maui" is an anticipation of the easy life ashore.

The whaler's life

In its many versions, "Off to Sea Once More" vividly portrays the real life of the whaler.

He shipped me aboard of a whaling ship, 'twas bound for the Arctic seas
Where the cold winds blow, and there's ice and snow, and Jamaica rum would freeze,
And worse to bear, I'd no hard weather gear, for I'd lost all me money ashore,
'Twas then that I wished that I was dead, so I'd go to sea no more.
Sometimes we're catching whales, me boys, and sometimes we catch none.
With a twenty-foot oar stuck in me hands from six o'clock in the morn,
And when at last the night comes on, I rest on my weary oar,
Oh a man must be blind to make up his mind fer to go to sea once more.

More recently, composers have written songs expressing their concerns about or delight in whales. Examples include Linda Waterfall's "The Whale Song," written after performing at a benefit concert for the Whale Museum in Friday Harbor and Raffi's "Baby Beluga," inspired by a visit to the Vancouver Aquarium. Sea World in San Diego even has a songbook targeted at children, featuring such titles as "Learning How to Swim Like a Whale" and "Dolphin and Me."

Paul Spong's insight—that if whales used echolocation they should respond to other musical stimuli—led to much experimentation in which whales became first the audience, then active partners. Early Greenpeace expeditions were enlivened by musicians who played flutes and saxes to whales from their boats. Paul Spong's home on Hanson Island became a base for experiments: rock bands playing from rafts, classical pieces broadcast from underwater speakers and joint improvisations with wild whales. During one of these sessions, Jim Nollman, a California musician, considered an orca taught him a song. "When a single orca issued a modulating, melodic phrase, I tried to copy it on the guitar. Then...the orca responded with an exact copy of my imperfect copy."

Paul Horn plays to the whales

Top: Paul Horn, jazz flautist and a founder of "new age" music, plays a duet with Haida. (Horn)

The jazz musician Paul Horn was one of the best known musicians to play with whales. Well known as jazz flute and sax player with the Chico Hamilton Quintet of California, Horn later made a series of experimental recordings inside such unusual settings as the Great Pyramid and Taj Mahal, a forerunner of what is now called New Age Music. In 1972 Paul Spong asked Horn—living in Victoria—to play for Sealand's orcas Haida and Chimo. By the third day the orcas were vocalizing in response.

Horn returned from a tour to find that Chimo had died, but played for Haida. Haida, apparently grieving, refused to eat and at first did not respond to the music. Eventually Horn broke through and established a rapport. "Haida really responded to my playing and seemed to favour the alto flute. He would lie on the water near me and occasionally answer back with a great variety of sounds from his blowhole." Horn planned to include joint improvisations on an album, but the recordings were too poorly recorded to release. In the studio he eventually improvised on flute to recordings of orca sounds. The resulting duet appeared on his album *Inside II.*

Totems and murals

First Nations made—and make—striking images of whales in stone, wood, cedar-bark in baskets and hats, button blankets, copper, silver and even whale bones. Some crude representations at least showed the power of the whale. Other images of great sophistication and beauty include a stunning Tlingit shaman's dolphin mask collected in Alaska by Edward Fast in the 1860s and now in the Peabody Museum at Harvard.

This pole, now in Vancouver's Stanley Park, is one of many that bears images of orcas, testifying to the importance of this whale in First Nations culture. (DAES)

Totem poles show many orcas and occasional gray whales; even poles of the inland Gitksan display images of blackfish and finback whales. The *Great Killer Whale* copper, once owned by Chief Mungo Martin of the Kwakwa'ka'wakw, bears a whale design. Sophisticated modern representations include Robert Davidson's (a Haida artist) talking stick presented to Pope John Paul II and Davidson's *Three Variations on Killer Whale Myths*, consisting of three totem poles mounted in the Pepsico Sculpture Park at Purchase, New York.

A wall offers a big enough surface to paint a whale properly, and many a museum and watering hole, supermarket and scuba shop features a cetacean subject. Several works by the "Whaling Wall" muralist Robert Wyland include a striking image in Victoria's downtown in tribute to the whale photographer Robin Morton. Far more are done by less-known artists, some of whom are unaware of the social structure of orca pods and present multiple versions of the same whale instead of a natural grouping.

The colourful subject of whaling attracted many a visual artist in the nineteenth century. With greater or lesser skill and accuracy, they rendered whaling ships, seascapes and incidents of the chase, with a particular fondness for flukes or jaws of the fierce sperm whale smashing frail boats. Whalers themselves found their trade an unending source of inspiration in their art of scrimshaw, engraving—as Melville put it—"lively sketches of whales and whaling-scenes" on sperm whale teeth and whale bones "in their hours of ocean leisure."

Wyland's "whaling wall," a building-sized mural, is a monument to whale photographer Robin Morton and a Victoria landmark. (DAES)

Logos and tattoos

For craftsmen and graphic designers, whales seem to be a source of unfailing fascination. The orca's black and white pattern makes it a particular favourite of those seeking a striking visual image. Orcas have inspired elegant logos for banks and publishers, a

Whale images turn up on mailboxes and signs, as well as many other applications ranging from business logos to tattoos. (DAES)

cartoon image for Klee Wyck, official mascot of the XV Commonwealth Games in Victoria, stencilled orcas decorating garbage containers in Alert Bay and a range of tattoos. Folk artists produce copper weathervanes, stained glass and a variety of other objects from elegant through cute to the kitsch of shop signs, mailboxes and mugs.

Freezing the action

Whale photography presents special challenges. The best work come from people who live around whales and have abundant opportunity to catch the elusive image. Whale researchers Ken Balcomb, Jim Darling, Graeme Ellis, John Ford and Alexandra Morton, and whale watching skipper Jim Borrowman, produce some of the most widely published work.

Kelly Balcomb-Bartok, the son of Ken Balcomb, was once known as "Kelly the killer whale kid." He saw his first orca at the age of five and has been with them almost ever since. "I know these whales better than I know my neighbours," said Kelly, who has taken some 5,000 colour photos of whales. He participates in Whale Research Center activities but also has his own photography gallery next to the Whale Museum in Friday Harbor.

Fact and fantasy on film

Several West Coast documentary films feature orcas or gray whales. Canada's National Film Board and the National Geographic Society have showcased these. Erich Hoyt has described several early 1970s seasons of filming orcas in his book *Orca: The Whale Called "Killer."* In 1987 a team from Jacques Cousteau's ship *Alcyone* filmed orcas at Alert Bay, and in 1995 a Japanese team flew into Telegraph Cove for just a few hours to get some footage. A spectacular IMAX film showing West Coast whales almost life-size was chosen to open the Royal British Columbia Museum's new IMAX theatre in June 1998.

Since the day of the TV series featuring the dolphin Flipper, whales have been a popular subject for fictional video and film. These reflect changing public perceptions. The 1970s *Orca* was a sort of mammalian *Jaws,* while in the recent *Free Willy* films the central cetacean is a rather anthropomorphized pal to the teenaged human hero. Stories with environmental themes are now popular—*Free Willy* alone grossed over $100 million.

Using swimming miniatures, a million-dollar animatronic whale, computer-generated images and the real thing, *Free Willy 2* was mainly filmed in and around the San Juan Islands of Washington state. Three years of field photography produced fine footage of wild orcas, which were computer-manipulated to maintain the appearance of flaccid-finned Keiko, who originally played Willy from his Mexican tank. The plot is fashionably environmental, with evil oilmen plotting to recapture Willy and his family for aquaria against the background of an *Exxon Valdez*-type oil spill. (For more on Keiko, see Chapter 8.)

Land of the war canoes

The first film to feature whales in the Pacific Northwest was one of the pioneer movies in the region and also one of the earliest to attempt to depict the reality of First Nations cultures.

American photographer Edward Curtis (celebrated for his twenty volumes of photographs of First Peoples) visited British Columbia in 1914 and extended the range of his photographic work by making a movie based on the life of the Kwakiutl (Kwakwa'ka'wakw) of northern Vancouver Island. Although noted as a documentary photographer, Curtis wanted to document traditions that seemed to be fast disappearing, which led him to fake many still shots, getting his subjects to pose in costumes and situations of an earlier era. The film, originally called *In the Land of the Head Hunters*, was briefly shown commercially and then disappeared. A print came to light in the late 1940s, however, and stills showing the filming emerged in 1977. Research by Bill Holm and George Quimby of Seattle's Burke Museum shows that Curtis also faked his movie in the interests of historic authenticity, showing First Nations actors in costumes and behaviour of the remembered past. Of course, he also developed a storyline in pursuit of what contemporary Hollywood considered box office success.

In 1967 Holm revisited the areas where Curtis filmed, showing the movie to locals and interviewing many who had participated in the filming. The Kwakiutl had had a whaling tradition in the Quatsino Sound area, but Curtis shot the film's whaling scenes at Naden Harbour in the Queen Charlottes, where he borrowed a dead whale from a whaling company and used Haida actors. Nevertheless, the aboriginal whaling scenes, showing a whale being brought in and cut up, reconstruct probable scenes on the coast in earlier times. The film has been reconstructed with the addition of a soundtrack; retitled *In the Land of the War Canoes*, it is shown from to time in museums.

Whale steak, anyone?

Discussing whales' role in the culinary arts is not politically correct today, but it played an integral part in the history of the human–cetacean relationship. First Nations not only ate the meat but flavoured many other foods with whale oil. Other cultures are familiar with whale meat as food—Japanese flensers at Coal Harbour would cut thin strips of meat and cook them on the machinery for snacks.

Whales played no traditional part in the diet of North America's nonaboriginal population, but there have been a number of attempts to change this pattern. "Whale meat is really good, if properly prepared, even to western taste," said Roy Chapman Andrews. Early in World War I, Andrews tried to popularize whale meat with a luncheon at the American Museum in New York. The meat was sent in refrigerated cars from Alaska and Vancouver Island to New York, Chicago, Seattle, San Francisco and other major cities in the USA. "It went well enough at first, but the expense of transporting it such long distances made the plan impracticable after the novelty wore off."

By 1919 the trade journal *Pacific Fisherman* was announcing that refrigerated or canned whale meat was available from Bay City, Washington. In Victoria it sold for 10 cents per pound; publication of recipes for Whale Meat Roll and Whale Meat Shepherd's Pie encouraged people to eat "sea beef." A dispute arose between butchers and fishmongers, however, as each felt that the other trade should carry the product. Whale meat was particularly popular in Boston, and in 1919 it was expected that 1,000 tons of frozen and 50,000 cases of canned whale meat would be distributed, "for all of which a market is assured."

Although mainstream society has not taken to sea beef, whalers—and their families—have never objected to the main source of fresh meat in their diet. "We all grew up on whale meat," said Darlene Cadwallader, a child in Coal Harbour during the whaling years," and we were fine healthy kids. Makes me feel a bit weird whale watching now."

Big bones and lively programs

The Marine Mammal Museum in Sidney, British Columbia and the Whale Museum in Friday Harbor, San Juan Island, are the major museums in the region celebrating the life of cetaceans. Here you will find skeletons and skulls, artifacts and information, staff and volunteers, all combining to create enlightening exhibits, a buzz of information and usually a centre of fundraising, education and research. Sidney's museum, which also houses local history, overlooks the shore. It has an impressive exhibit, a useful research library and a small but well-stocked shop.

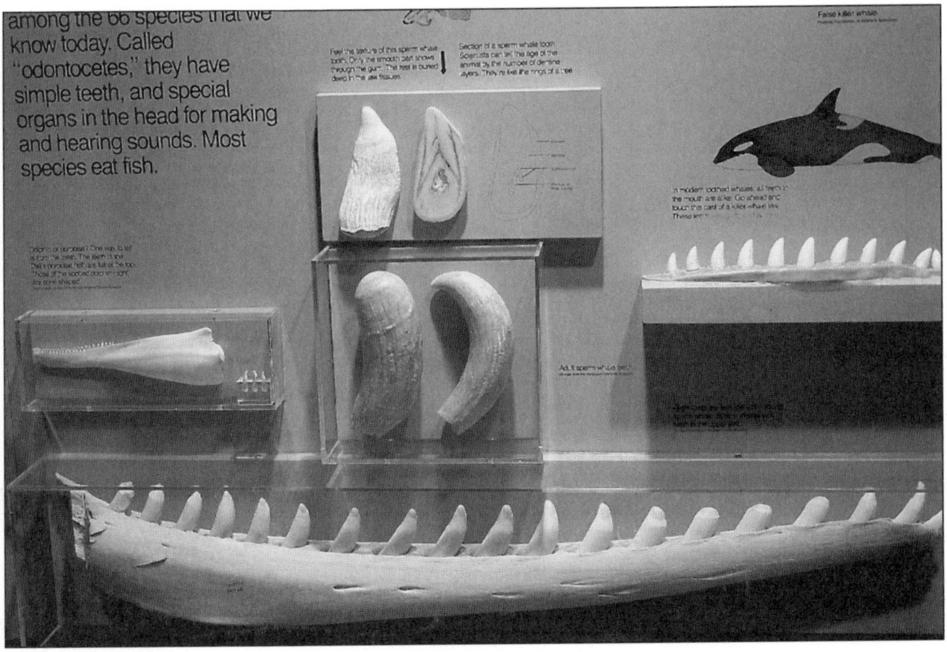

The whale exhibit at Vancouver Aquarium interprets aspects of the story that cannot be illustrated by living whales. (DAES)

The Whale Museum at Friday Harbor is the San Juan Islands' biggest tourist draw. Started in the late 1970s by Ken Balcomb and Mark Anderson, it runs whale research and education programs—including whale watching trips—with the support of 400 volunteers. It occupies an 1893 Oddfellows Hall at the top of a hill, a prominent landmark, and its shop offers a wonderful selection of whale books. The smaller Whale Centre in Tofino exhibits local whale material.

Other museums feature whales too. Anthropological museums exhibit First Nations artifacts and feature whales as part of the culture, while maritime museums present the story of whaling as part of the overall story of ships and the sea. Larger general museums such as the Burke Museum in Seattle and the Royal British Columbia Museum in Victoria feature all aspects of the life of the region, not neglecting whales. During its first years in its current building, the Royal's entrance hall displayed a larger-than-life sculpture of a group of Nuu-chah-nulth whalers about to lance a gray whale. A team of First Nations sculptors created the carving in wood. The museum has kept the sculpture in storage since remodelling the entrance hall. In 1997 it brought together a major temporary exhibit, *Whales: The Enduring Legacy*, which ran for a year.

Some of these museums run lively whale-related programs, playing an important public education role and raising funds for research and conservation. In the Pacific Northwest, both the Vancouver Aquarium and the Whale Museum run whale adoption programs, among the most creative ways of raising both the profile of whales and money to further whale research. Successfully running in Canada, the USA and England, these fundraising programs give interested members of the public around the world a personal stake in studying and protecting whale populations. In our region you can adopt an orca; programs elsewhere offer belugas, blue, fin, humpback and right whales and spotted dolphins for adoption.

Orca adoption programs became possible once researchers could identify and name not only the pods but individual pod members, and provide descriptions and photos of their dorsal fins and saddle patch markings—each as unique to the individual orca as a fingerprint is to an individual human.

Orca Adoption Program

You, your family, your school or other organization can adopt a whale. After choosing from the sponsoring organization's list, for an adoption fee you receive an identification photo of your whale, its family history and a series of newsletters updating you on the pod's movements—including sightings of your adoptee—for a one-year period. The newsletter information generally comes from research your money is funding. Programs and adoption kits differ slightly from place to place. At the Whale Museum in Friday Harbor, San Juan Islands, the adopter can get not only information on a particular whale but an adoption certificate with its photo, official and informal names, a discount at the museum store, museum membership for a year—with a quarterly newsletter on current research—and a video of the National Geographic Special *Killer Whales: Wolves of the Sea.*

About 16,000 people now support research programs through the Friday Harbor Whale Museum Adopt-A-Whale program, started in 1984 and run by volunteers."This is such a rewarding job," volunteer Consuelo Larrabee smiled as she stuck identification photos on a certificate for a new supporter. "I feel I'm sending out information about a member of my own family." She was so sincere and enthusiastic that she signed us up by the end of the conversation; we chose Dylan, profiled in Chapter 3. (Look for addresses of adopt-a-whale programs in Resources.) —AJS

The Pacific Northwest attracts interest from nonprofit organizations based farther south and even overseas. For example, whale watching tours from the American Cetacean Society and the Ocean Society—both based in California—give members first-hand experiences of whales in the wild and help to raise funds for the organizations' work. The British Whale and Dolphin Centre for Research has also actively funded West Coast research, supporting work by Alexandra Morton and the Center for Whale Research.

How you can help

- Record your own observations
- Report sightings of whales on whale hotlines
- Adopt a whale of your own
- Join and volunteer for whale study and conservation organizations
- Go and see whales for yourself

For further information on various organizations, see Resources.

Resources

Whale words

This book uses some special words commonly used to describe whales:

Baleen—fibrous horny plates hanging from the roof of the mouth in baleen whales, used to trap small food animals (also known misleadingly as whalebone).

Barnacles—a group of crustaceans (related to crabs), some species of which live on the outsides of whales.

Blow—the spout of the whale. ("Thar she blows!")

Blowhole—the nostrils of the whale, a single or double opening on top of the skull.

Blubber—a layer of fat beneath the skin.

Cetacea—the order of mammals to which all whales belong.

Cetologist—a whale scientist.

Dorsal fin—a cartilaginous, more or less triangular plate, which projects from the back of most whales.

Echolocation—a method of location used by some of the smaller whales, which make sounds and listen for their echoes.

Flippers—the front limbs of the whale, which have evolved into flat paddles.

Flukes—the whale's tail, often shown when it dives.

Friendly—a whale which seeks and appears to enjoy human company.

Krill—planktonic crustaceans an inch or two (2.5 to 5 cm) long, shoals of which provide food for some baleen whales.

Lobtailing—slapping the surface with raised flukes.

Melon—the bulbous forehead of some toothed whales, which focusses sounds used in echolocation.

Mysticete—a baleen whale (e.g. gray). From the Greek for "moustached whale."
Odontocete—a toothed whale (e.g. orca).
Plankton—animals (including krill) and plants that float in the sea.
Spermaceti—the oil in the reservoir in the head of the sperm whale.
Spout—a puff of water vapour, visible when a whale breathes out (at or close to the surface).
Spyhopping—lifting the head vertically out of the water.
Whalebone—baleen; it is made not of bone but of keratin, a substance like our fingernails.
Whale lice—a group of crustaceans (a group including crabs) that are parasites of whales.

Whales through time

The story of whales in the Pacific Northwest began some 65 million years ago, when the Cretaceous extinction removed potentially competing marine reptiles from the oceans. Fossil whales are found in the area, and bones in archaeological sites show that whales were eaten, and perhaps caught, more than a thousand years ago.

Commercial whaling has been important to the region's economy at least since contact between First Nations, Europeans and new North Americans, and culminated in extensive shore-based whaling in the twentieth century.

Since the mid-nineteenth century, scientific study at first depended on the whalers, then grew independently. For a time, as the world's only source of captive orcas, the area triggered conservation efforts that have successfully addressed some problems affecting whales worldwide. We are only beginning to recognize other problems in science and conservation.

Abbreviations:

AK = Alaska; BC = British Columbia; BP = before present; IWC = International Whaling Commission; my = million years ago; QCI = Queen Charlotte Islands (Haida Gwaii); UNEP = United Nations Environmental Protection agency; VI = Vancouver Island; WA = Washington state.

The geological past

65 my—End of Cretaceous extinction of marine reptiles makes the ocean safe for whales.

50 my—Eocene Epoch has first fossil whales.

35 my—Oligocene Epoch has whales in Pacific Northwest; toothed and baleen whales are distinct.

Human prehistory

1200 BP—Toggle harpoons big enough for whaling used at Yuquot, VI.

Sixteenth century

c. 1525—Basques whaling off Newfoundland.

c. 1580—Mudslide preserves First Nations whaling village at Ozette, WA.

Eighteenth century

1778—Captain James Cook arrives at Nootka Sound, VI and encounters the Nuu-chah-nulth whaling culture.

1784–85—Publication of Cook's *Voyages* draws attention to whales in Pacific.

1788—British whaler *Emelia* rounds the Horn, hunts off Chile.

1790—Nootka convention formally opens northwest waters to English whalers.

1791–93—Forty whaling ships in South Pacific pursue sperm whales.

1792—Brown trades for whale products in the QCI.

Nineteenth century

1803—John Jewitt observes whaling culture at Nootka, VI.

1834—First British whaler off northwest coast.

1835—Pacific whalers begin to take bowheads off Alaska.

1838–42—US Exploring Expedition explores Pacific.

1846—Shore-based whaling for gray whales begins in California.

1851—400 ships take right whales on Kodiak Ground.

1852—Charles Scammon goes to sea in command of a whaling brig.

1856—Swan observes First Nations with dead whale near Gray's Harbor, WA.

1864—Svend Foyn invents modern harpoon gun.

1866—James Dawson hunts humpbacks in Saanich Inlet, VI.

1874—Scammon publishes *Marine Mammals of the Northwestern Coasts of North America.*
1880—Steam whaler *Mary D. Hume* operates in Northwest from San Francisco.
1881—*Mary D. Hume* is launched in Oregon.
1883—Stejneger finds beaked whale on Bering Island, AK.
1886—British Columbia Provincial Museum opens.
1898—Samuel Foyn tries to start whaling in British Columbia.

Twentieth century

1904—Canadian government passes legislation requiring licensing of whaling stations.
—Commercial shore whaling begins on the west coast of VI.
—George Hunt acquires whaler's shrine.
1907—Admiralty Island, AK whaling station opens.
—Whale watching in Howe Sound, BC.
—Humpback whaling begins from Page's Lagoon near Nanaimo, VI.
1908—Roy Chapman Andrews visits Sechart, VI.
1910—Makah whaling is photographed on Washington coast.
1911—"Rainbow" fleet arrives in Victoria, BC, from Norway.
—Port Armstrong opens on Baranof Island near Sitka, AK.
1912—Akutan whaling station opens in the Aleutians, AK.
1913—President William Taft protects wildlife in Aleutians, AK.
1914—Edward Curtis films in British Columbia.
1914–18—World War I creates demand for whale products.
1916—Andrews *Whale Hunting with Gun and Camera* is published.
1919—Refrigerated and canned whale meat available.
1937—Minke skeleton becomes first whale in British Columbia Provincial Museum.
—International whaling agreement is signed by most nations.
—Victor Scheffer joins the US Biological Survey.
1939—Shore whaling is closed down in Alaska.
1946—International Convention for the Regulation of Whaling is established.
—Clifford Carl tracks an albino orca.
1948—Coal Harbour station is established.
1951—Canada Whaling Convention Act is passed.
1955—Modern whale watching begins in California.
1956—Vancouver Aquarium opens.

1959—Canadian Department of Fisheries and Oceans mounts a machine gun to kill orcas.
1961—Gray whales recover to about 6,000.
1963—Hubbs' beaked whale becomes the most recent new species named in the region.
1964—Vancouver aquarium catches first captive orca.
1965—Namu, an orca accidentally caught in a net, is displayed at Seattle.
1966—Excavations under way at Makah whaler's village.
—Vancouver Aquarium acquires Pacific white-sided dolphins.
1967—Paul Spong researching at the Vancouver Aquarium.
—Coal Harbour, last active shore whaling station, closes.
1968—Individual humpbacks are documented in Alaska.
—Sealand's first orca, Haida, arrives at Oak Bay, VI.
1969—*Marine Mammals of British Columbia* is published.
1970—Michael Bigg begins orca research.
1971—First orca census takes place.
1972—UN Conference on Human Environment recommends ten-year moratorium on whaling.
—Canada bans whaling from Canadian ports.
—US passes Marine Mammal Protection Act.
—Paul Horn plays for orcas at Sealand, Oak Bay, VI.
1973—Mike Bigg begins photo identification of orcas.
—Spong encourages Greenpeace to protest whaling.
—Convention on International Trade in Endangered Species is established.
—US passes Endangered Species Act.
1974—Graeme Ellis begins work with Michael Bigg.
1975—Greenpeace intervenes in Russian whaling.
1976—San Juan Center for Whale Research opens, WA.
—Ken Balcomb starts annual orca census in Washington state waters.
—Humpback tagging begins in Alaska.
—US passes Fisheries Conservation Management Act.
1977—John Ford begins whale vocalization studies.
1978—Alexandra Morton begins research on orcas.
1979—Mass sperm whale stranding occurs at Florence, Oregon.
1980—Commercial whale watching begins in Johnstone Strait, BC.
1981—Canada withdraws from International Whaling Commission.
1982—Robson Bight ecological reserve is established, VI.

—IWC agrees to a moratorium on whaling.
1983—Whale Watching Park is dedicated on San Juan Island, WA.
1984—Bill Reid sculpture is unveiled at Vancouver Aquarium.
1986—Vancouver Aquarium opens Max Bell Marine Mammal Centre.
1987—The first popular summary of orca research, Bigg's *Killer Whales*, is published.
1988—First orca is born in captivity in Canada.
—Greenpeace receives an award from UNEP.
1992—Sealand of the Pacific shuts down, Oak Bay, VI.
—Oregon Coast Aquarium opens.
1994—New US Marine Mammal Protection Act is passed.
1996—Keiko is moved to a new pool in Newport, Oregon.
1998—Keiko is moved to Iceland.
—Makah begin whaling off Washington coast.

Through the seasons

(provinces and states are listed north to south)

January
Alaska: Whales can be seen by the hardy viewer.
Oregon: Last gray whale southward migration begins.
California: Gray whales migrating south.

February
Washington: First grays move north.
Oregon: First grays move north.
California: Gray whales.

March
Alaska: Gray whales first pass Kodiak Island.
BC: Gray whales appear off Tofino and Queen Charlotte Islands; Pacific Rim Whale Festival begins.
Washington: Gray whale watching begins on outer coast.
Oregon: Gray whales head north.
California: Gray whales head north.

April
Alaska: Gray whales pass Sitka.
BC: Gray whale northward migration reaches its peak.
Washington: Gray whale northward migration reaches its peak; orca watching starts in San Juans.
Oregon: Gray whale northward migration continues.

California: Gray whale migration off northern shores.

May

Alaska: Gray whale watching continues.

BC: Resident grays may be seen, and last of northbound grays pass.

Washington: Last of northbound grays depart, orca watching active in San Juans and Gulf Islands.

Oregon: Resident grays may be seen.

California: Gray whale mothers and calves may be seen.

June

Alaska: Whale watching is active; fin whales arrive at Kodiak Island.

BC: Watching of resident grays; orcas in Johnstone Strait and Gulf Islands.

Washington: Orca watching reaches peak in San Juans and Puget Sound.

Oregon: Resident grays may be seen.

July

Alaska: Season is in full swing, fin and sei whales may be seen at Kodiak Island.

BC: Watching of Johnstone Strait and Gulf Islands orcas and Pacific Rim resident grays.

Washington: Orca watching in San Juans, Puget Sound.

Oregon: Resident grays and orcas may be seen.

California: Sperm whales off the coast.

August

Alaska: Orca concentration is highest at Kodiak Island.

BC: Watching of resident grays at Tofino, orcas in Johnstone Strait and Gulf Islands.

Washington: Orca watching in San Juans, Puget Sound.

Oregon: Resident grays may be seen.

California: Blue whales off the coast.

September

Alaska: Most whale watching ends.

BC: Some resident grays remain at Pacific Rim; orca watching still active in Johnstone Strait and Gulf Islands.

Washington: Orca watching is still active in San Juans, Puget Sound.

Oregon: Resident grays may be seen.

California: Blue and humpback whales off the coast.

October

Alaska: Best humpback watching at Sitka begins.

BC: Gray whale watching ends, orca watching in Johnstone Strait ends.
Washington: Most operators close down.
Oregon: Resident grays may still be seen.
November
Alaska: Humpbacks are most active round Kodiak Island.
Oregon: Gray southbound migration begins.
December
Alaska: Humpbacks around.
Oregon: Gray southbound migration continues.
California: Gray southbound migration continues.

Information for travellers

Outside visitors coming to the West Coast can get information about transportation and accommodation from provincial and state tourist agencies. They will give you more detailed information about whale watching and direct you to local information sources. Don't forget to add the country to your address—Canada (for British Columbia) or USA (for Alaska, California, Oregon, Washington). Many general guidebooks are available for the region.

Alaska Division of Tourism, PO Box 110801, Juneau, AK 99811-0806, tel (907) 465-2010, fax (907) 465-2287, http://www.travelalaska.com/

Tourism British Columbia, 1117 Wharf Street, Victoria, BC V8W 2Z2, tel (604) 387-1428, Discover BC (800) 663-6000, http://www.bc-tourism.com/

Washington State Tourism Development Division, PO Box 42500, Olympia, WA 98504-2500, tel (800) 544-1800, http://www.tourism.wa.gov/

Oregon Economic Development Department, Tourism Division, 775 Summer St. NE, Salem, OR 97310, tel (800) 547-7842, (800) 543-8838, http://www.traveloregon.com/

California Division of Tourism, 801 K Street, Suite 1600, Sacramento, CA 95814, tel (800) TO-CALIF, http://gocalif.ca.gov/

Adopt a Whale

If you'd like to help research programs by adopting your own whale:

Blue whales

Oceanic Society, Fort Mason Center, Building E, San Francisco, CA 94123, tel (800) 326-7491

Gray whales

Tarlton Institute for Marine Education, 50 Francisco Street, Suite 103, San Francisco, CA 94133, tel (415) 433-3163

Humpback whales

Oceanic Society, Fort Mason Center, Building E, San Francisco, CA 94123, tel (800) 326-7491

Orcas

Northern residents and transients:

Killer Whale Adoption Program, Vancouver Aquarium, PO Box 3232, Vancouver, BC V6B 3X8, tel (604) 631-2516, fax (604) 631-2529, http://www.killerwhale.org/

Southern residents:

Orca Adoption Program, The Whale Museum, 62 First Street North, PO Box 945, Friday Harbor, WA 98250, tel (360) 378-4710, fax (360) 378-5790, http://www.whale-museum.org/

Aquaria

Cetaceans are usually shown at:

BC

Vancouver Aquarium Marine Science Centre, PO Box 3232, Stanley Park, Vancouver, BC V6B 3X8, tel (604) 685-3364, http://www.vanaqua.org/

Oregon

Oregon Coast Aquarium, 2820 SE Ferry Slip Rd., Newport, OR 97365, tel (503) 867-3474, fax (503) 867-6846, http://www.aquarium.org/

Washington

Point Defiance Zoo and Aquarium at Tacoma, 5400 North Pearl Street, Tacoma, WA 98407, tel (206) 591-5337

Museums, exhibits and festivals

Alaska

Pratt Museum, 3779 Bartlett Street, Homer, AK 99603, tel (907) 235-8635

University of Alaska Museum, 907 Yukon Drive, Fairbanks, AK 99775, tel (907) 474-7505, fax (907) 474-5469

BC

Sidney Museum, 2440 Sidney Avenue, Sidney, BC V8L 1Y7, tel (250) 656-2140 (marine mammal exhibits)

Whale Centre, 411 Campbell Street, PO Box 393, Tofino, BC V0R 2Z0, tel (250) 725-3163

Pacific Rim Whale Festival, Box 948, Ucluelet, BC V0R 3A0, tel (250) 726-7336

Wickaninnish Centre, Pacific Rim National Park, PO Box 280, Ucluelet, BC V0R 3A0, tel (250) 726-7721

Museum of Anthropology, 6393 NW Marine Drive, Vancouver, BC V6T 1W5, tel (604) 228-3825

Vancouver Maritime Museum, 1905 Ogden Avenue, Vancouver, BC V6J 1A3, tel (604) 257-8306, fax (604) 737-2621

Maritime Museum of BC, 28 Bastion Square, Victoria, BC V8W 2H9, tel (250) 385-4222

Royal British Columbia Museum, 672 Belleville Street, Victoria, BC V8V 1X4, tel (250) 387-3014

Washington

Makah Cultural & Research Center, P.O. Box 160, Neah Bay, WA 98357, tel (360) 645-2711

Westport Maritime Museum, 2201 Westhaven Drive, P.O. Box 1074, Westport, WA 98595-1074, tel (360) 268-0078

The Whale Museum, 62 First Street North, Friday Harbor, WA 98250, tel (206) 378-4710 http://www.whale-museum.org/

Festival of Whales (May) The Whale Museum

Oregon

Mark O. Hatfield Marine Science Center, Oregon State University, 2030 South Marine Science Drive, Newport, OR 97365, tel (503) 867-0100

California

A number of centres, such as Santa Barbara, hold Festivals of Whales to coincide with their local gray whale migrations, while leading museums run their own whale watching trips.

Cabrillo Marine Aquarium, 3720 Stephen White Drive, San Pedro, CA 90731, tel (213) 548-7562

California Academy of Science, Golden Gate Park, San Francisco, CA 94118, tel (415) 221-5100, fax (415) 750-7346

Long Marine Laboratory, 100 Shaffer Road, Santa Cruz, CA 95060, tel (408) 459-4308, fax (408) 459-3383

Monterey Bay Aquarium, 886 Cannery Row, Monterey, CA 93940, tel (408) 648-4800

San Diego Natural History Museum, P.O Box 1390, Balboa Park, San Diego, CA 91112, tel (619) 232-3821

Santa Barbara Museum of Natural History, 2559 Puesta del Sol Road, Santa Barbara, CA 93105, tel (805) 682-4711

Stephen Birch Aquarium, Scripps Institute of Oceanography, 2300 Expedition Way, La Jolla, CA 92093, tel (619) 534-3474, fax (619) 534-7114

Parks

Alaska

Glacier Bay National Park & Preserve, PO Box 140, Gustavus, AK 99826, tel (907) 697-2231

Kenai Fjords National Park, National Park Service, 540 West 5th Avenue, Anchorage, AK 99501, tel (907) 224-3175

BC

Robson Bight Ecological Reserve, BC Parks, Strathcona District, Rathtrevor Beach Park, Parksville, BC V0R 2S0, tel (250) 248-3931

Pacific Rim National Park, Box 280, Ucluelet, BC V0R 3A0, tel (250) 726-7721

Washington

Lime Kiln Park is a favourite whale watching site.

Olympic National Park, 600 E. Park Avenue, Port Angeles, WA 98362-6798, tel (206) 452-4501

Oregon

All coastal parks offer the opportunities to see gray whales: Cape Arago and Port Orford Wayside State Parks are among the best.

California
A number of parks, marine sanctuaries and national monuments offer whale watching opportunities, notably Point Reyes National Seashore, Point Reyes, CA 94959, (415) 663-1092.

Whale hotlines and photo archives

BC
Strandings: report to Whale Reporting and Stranding Report Line, tel (800)-665-5939
or: Marine Mammal Research Group, PO Box 6244, Victoria, BC V8P 5L5, tel (250) 380-1925, fax (250) 380-1206
Marine mammal harassment: report to Department of Fisheries and Oceans, tel (800) 465-4336
Send photos to Marine Mammal Research, Department of Fisheries and Oceans, Pacific Biological Station, Nanaimo, BC V9R 5K6, tel (250) 756-7245
Washington
Sightings and strandings: report to whale hotline, tel (800) 562-8832
Marine mammal harassment: report to National Marine Fisheries Service, tel (206) 526-6133, (360) 676-9268
or: Center for Whale Research, PO Box 1577, Friday Harbor, WA 98250, tel (206) 378-5835
Oregon
For whale watching information, phone (541) 563-2002

Whale research and conservation agencies

Most museums are also involved in research and conservation.
Alaska
North Gulf Oceanic Society, PO Box 15244, Homer, AK 99603
BC
Strawberry Island Research, Box 213, Tofino, BC V0R 2Z0
Washington
Center for Whale Research, 1359 Smugglers Cove, Friday Harbor, WA 98250
People for Puget Sound, 1326 Fifth Avenue, #450, Seattle, WA 98101, or P.O. Box 2807, Seattle, WA 98111-9912

Oregon
Mark O. Hatfield Marine Science Center, Oregon State University, 2030 South Marine Science Drive, Newport, OR 97365, tel (503) 867-0100
Other
American Cetacean Society, PO Box 2639, San Pedro, CA 90731, http://www.acsonline.org/
Delilah Fund for Whale Conservation, World Wildlife Fund Canada, 90 Eglinton Ave. E. Suite 504, Toronto, ON M4P 2Z7
Earthwatch, 680 Mount Auburn Street, Box 403 N, Watertown, MA 02272, tel (800) 776-0188, (616) 926-8200

Whale watching

It is not possible to list here even a fraction of the 150 or so whale watching outfits on the Pacific coast. The best sources of specific information are recent whale watching guides (see Resources) and regional tourist information centres in places where whale watching takes place. Most whale watching trips go from relatively few ports (listed below): with the help of provincial and state tourist agencies (some of whom have special whale watching listings) this information should get you fairly quickly to the contacts you need to plan a trip.
Alaska
Anchorage, Gustavus, Haines, Juneau, Ketchikan, Kodiak, Petersburg, Seward, Sitka, Valdez, Wrangell
BC
Alert Bay, Bamfield, Campbell River, Courtenay, Delta, Kitimat, Nanaimo, Port Alberni, Port Hardy, Port McNeill, Prince Rupert, Queen Charlotte City, Sandspit, Saturna Island, Sayward, Sidney, Sointula, Sooke, Telegraph Cove, Tofino, Ucluelet, Vancouver, Victoria
Washington
Aberdeen, Anacortes, Auburn, Bellingham, Deer Harbor, Eastsound, Everett, Friday Harbor, Ilwaco, La Conner, La Push, Orcas, Port Townsend, Roche Harbor, Seattle, Vashon, Westport
Oregon
"Whale Watching Spoken Here" at 28 sites.
Brookings, Charleston, Depoe Bay, Eugene, Florence, Garibaldi, Lincoln City, Newport, Winchester Bay

California

Avila Beach, Balboa, Berkeley, Dana Point, Fort Bragg, Half Moon Bay, Long Beach, Monterey, Morro Bay, Newport Beach, Oceanside, Oxnard, Point Arena, Redondo Beach, San Diego, San Francisco, San Pedro, Santa Barbara, Santa Cruz, Ventura

Recommended reading

Many books mention whales of the Pacific Northwest, but they are the primary subject of only a few, listed here. Most books recommended are recent (and likely available), except for a small number of classics to be found in libraries and used bookstores.

Biography

Newman, Murray. *Life in a Fishbowl: Confessions of an Aquarium Director.* Vancouver: Douglas & McIntyre, 1994.

Scheffer, Victor B. *Adventures of a Zoologist.* New York: Charles Scribner's Sons, 1980.

Classics

Andrews, Roy Chapman. *Whale Hunting with Gun and Camera: A Naturalist's Account of the Modern Shore-Whaling Industry, of Whales and Their Habits, and of Hunting Experiences in Various Parts of the World.* D. Appleton & Company, 1916, 1931.

Haig-Brown, Roderick. *The Whale People.* Toronto: Totem, 1962.

Pike, Gordon C. and Ian McAskie. *Marine Mammals of British Columbia.* Fisheries Research Board Bulletin 171, 1969.

Scammon, C. M. (1874) *The Marine Mammals of the North-Western Coast of North America, Described and Illustrated: Together with an account of the American Whale Fishery.* New York: Dover, 1968.

Conservation

Hamilton, Peter. *Orca: A Family Story.* Vancouver: Lifeforce Foundation, 1993.

Weyler, Rex. *Song of the Whale.* New York: Anchor/Doubleday, 1986.

Grays

Busch, Robert H. *Gray Whales, Wandering Giants.* Victoria: Orca, 1998.

Gordon and Baldridge. *Gray Whales.* Monterey Bay Aquarium, 1991.

Fiction

Gough, Laurence. *Killers.* Toronto: McClelland & Stewart, 1994.

Scheffer, V. B. *The Year of the Whale.* New York: Charles Scribner's Sons, 1969.

Humpbacks

D'Vincent, Cynthia. *Voyaging with the Whales.* Toronto: McClelland & Stewart, 1989.

Orcas

Ford, John K. B., Graeme M. Ellis, Kenneth C. Balcomb. *Killer Whales: The natural history and genealogy of Orcinus orca in British Columbia and Washington State.* Vancouver/Seattle: UBC Press/University of Washington Press, 1994.

Hand, Douglas. *Gone Whaling: A Search for Orcas in Northwest Waters.* New York: Simon & Schuster, 1994.

Hoyt, Erich. *Orca: The Whale Called "Killer."* Buffalo, NY. Camden House, 1990.

Knutson, Peter. *Orca: Visions of the Killer Whale.* Vancouver: Douglas & McIntyre, 1996.

Matkin, Craig. *An Observer's Guide to the Killer Whales of Prince William Sound.* Valdez, Alaska: Prince William Sound Books, 1994.

Morton, Alexandra. *Siwiti—A Whale's Story.* Victoria: Orca, 1991.

Morton, Alexandra. *In the Company of Whales: From the Diary of a Whale Watcher.* Victoria: Orca, 1993.

Regional

Obee, Bruce & Graeme Ellis. *Guardians of the Whales: The Quest to Study Whales in the Wild.* North Vancouver: Whitecap Books, 1992.

Osborne, R. W., J. Calambokidis, Eleanor M. Dorsey. *Marine Mammals of Greater Puget Sound: a naturalist's field guide.* Anacortes, WA: Island Publications, 1988.

Yates, Steve. *Orcas, Eagles & Kings: A Popular Natural History of Georgia Strait and Puget Sound.* Seattle: Primavera Press, 1992.

Whale Watching

Corrigan, Patricia. *The Whale Watcher's Guide: Whale-watching trips in North America.* Northword Press, 1994.

Kreitman, Richard C. and Mary Jane Schramm. *West Coast Whale Watching: The Complete Guide to Observing Marine Mammals.* HarperCollins West, 1995.

Whaling

Goddard, Joan. *A Window on Whaling in British Columbia.* Jonah Publications, 1997.

Hagelund, W. A. *Whalers No More. A History of Whaling on the West Coast.* Madeira Park, BC: Harbour Publishing, 1987.

Webb, Robert L. *On the Northwest. Commercial Whaling in the Pacific Northwest 1790–1967.* Vancouver: UBC Press, 1988.

Periodicals

Many general interest, natural history, regional and specialized periodicals have articles on whales. In addition to the newsletters of whale-related organizations, important ones include *Canadian Geographic, Equinox, International Wildlife, National Geographic, Natural History, Nature Canada, Smithsonian,* and *Whalewatcher.*

Audio

Songs and Sounds of the Humpback Whale (Holborne Distributing Ltd., P.O. Box 309, Mount Albert, ON L0G 1M0), 1987.

Ford, John. *Blackfish Sound: Underwater Communication of Killer Whales in British Columbia.* VACD 900, 1992.

Video

National Film Board. *We Call Them Killers* (16 mins.), 1987.

National Film Board. *Island of Whales,* 1989.

National Film Board. *Washing of Tears* (55 mins.), 1994.

National Geographic Society. *Killer Whales: Wolves of the Sea* (60 mins.), 1993.

Photographic Credits

HISTORIC IMAGES
American Museum of Natural History
BC Archives and Records Service (BCARS)
Bancroft Library
Maritime Museum of British Columbia
Vancouver Maritime Museum (VMM)

CONTEMPORARY IMAGES
Key: Altleo: Wilfred Atleo; Baird: Robin Baird; Dennis: Steve Dennis; Dorst: Adrian Dorst; Ellis: Graeme Ellis; Folkens: Pieter Folkens; Goedert: Jim & Gail Goedert; Hole: Harry and Pat Hole; Horn: Paul Horn; Hua: Terry Hua; Maloff: Wayne Maloff; McTaggart-Cowan: Ian McTaggart-Cowan; Morton: Alexandra Morton; Morton R: Robin Morton; Pitman: Robert L. Pitman; Pusser: Todd Pusser; Sargeant: William Sarjeant: AJS: Andrea Spalding; DAES: David A.E. Spalding; Ursus: Ursus Photography; Weyler: Rex Weyler.

The screened-back humpback whale photo that appears on the opening page for each chapter is by Graeme Ellis/Ursus Photography.

Index

Other Outdoor, Science & Nature Books from HARBOUR PUBLISHING

The Beachcomber's Guide to Seashore Life in the Pacific Northwest

Duane Sept

The 274 most common animals and plants to be seen along the saltwater shores of the Pacific Northwest are described here. Packed with expert information but wonderfully accessible to any interested layperson, this book is perfect for a family or a school group, a Saturday beachwalker or a naturalists' club.

ISBN 1-55017-204-2 • 188 pages • 5½ x 8½ • 200 colour photos • $21.95 paper

Lake, River and Sea-Run Fishes of Canada

Frederick H. Wooding

The only popular guide to freshwater fishes in all parts of Canada, this book is a must for naturalists, anglers and anyone who loves fine nature writing. This revised edition includes a foreword by Professor Joseph Nelson of the University of Alberta and an updated essay on endangered species by Dr. R.R. Campbell.

ISBN 1-55017-175-5 • 304 pages • 6 x 9 • 36 colour illustrations, 14 line drawings, index • $18.95 paper

Shells & Shellfish of the Pacific Northwest

Rick M. Harbo

This comprehensive, easy-to-follow, full-colour guide introduces more than 250 species of mollusks—the clams, oysters, scallops, mussels, abalone, snails, limpets, tuskshells and chitons found along the beaches and intertidal and shallow waters of the Pacific Northwest.

ISBN 1-55017-146-1 • 272 pages • 5½ x 8½ • 350 colour photos, index • $24.95 paper

Coastal Fishes of the Pacific Northwest

Andy Lamb & Phil Edgell

Written by a marine biologist and illustrated in colour by a prize-winning underwater photographer, this is the only comprehensive field guide to marine fishes of BC, Washington and southern Alaska.

ISBN 0-920080-75-8 • 224 pages • 5½ x 8½ • index • $21.95 paper

These titles available at your local bookstore or from

HARBOUR PUBLISHING
P.O. Box 219, Madeira Park, BC, Canada V0N 2H0
Toll-Free Order Line: 1-800-667-2988
Fax: 604-883-9451 • E-mail: harbour@sunshine.net